GETTING A BUSINESS LOAN:

Your

Step-By-Step

Guide

by Orlando J. Antonini

CREDITS

Editor: Beverly Manber

Layout/Design: University Graphics

Cover Design: Kathleen Gadway

Copyright ©1993 Crisp Publications

Library of Congress 92-54353
ISBN-1-56052-164-3

Limits of Liability and Disclaimer of Warranty

The author and publisher have used their best efforts in preparing this book and make no warranty of any kind, expressed or implied, with regard to the instructions and suggestions contained herein. This book is not intended to render legal or accounting advice. Such advice should be obtained from competent, licensed professionals.

INTRODUCTION TO THE SERIES

This series of books is intended to inform and assist those of you who are in the beginning stages of starting a new small business venture or who are considering such an undertaking.

It is because you are confident of your abilities that you are taking this step. These books will provide additional information and support along the way.

Not every new business will succeed. The more information you have about budgeting, cash flow management, accounts receivables, marketing and employee management, the better prepared you will be for the inevitable pitfalls.

A unique feature of the *Crisp Small Business & Entrepreneurship Series* is the personal involvement exercises, which give you many opportunities to immediately apply the concepts presented to your own business.

In each book in the series, these exercises take the form of "Your Turn", a checklist to confirm your understanding of the concept just presented and "Ask Yourself…", a series of chapter-ending questions, designed to evaluate your overall understanding or commitment.

In addition, numerous case studies are included, and each book is cross-referenced to others in the series and to other publications.

BOOKS IN THE SERIES

- **Operating a Really Small Business**
  Betty M. Bivins

- **Budgeting: A Primer for Entrepreneurs**
  Terry Dickey

- **Getting a Business Loan: Your Step-By-Step Guide**
  Orlando J. Antonini

- **Nobody Gets Rich Working for Somebody Else: An Entrepreneur's Guide**
  Roger Fritz

- **Marketing Strategies for Small Business**
  Richard F. Gerson, Ph.D.

- **Financial Basics for Small Business Success**
  James O. Gill

- **Extending Credit and Collecting Cash: A Small Business Guide**
  Lynn Harrison

- **Avoiding Mistakes in Your New Business**
  David Karlson, Ph.D.

- **Buying Your First Franchise: The Least You Need to Know**
  Rebecca Luhn, Ph.D.

- **Buying a Business: Tips for the First-Time Buyer**
  Ronald J. McGregor

- **Your New Business: A Personal Plan for Success**
  Charles L. Martin, Ph.D.

- **Managing the Family Business: A Guide for Success**
  Marshall W. Northington, Ph.D.

CONTENTS

CHAPTER ONE — PREPARING FOR THE LENDING PROCESS 1
   A Wide Variety of Loans 3
   A Wide Variety of Lenders 4
   The Key is Preparation 7
   Advance Planning Can Make the Difference 14

CHAPTER TWO — ORGANIZING YOUR LOAN PROPOSAL 17
   Knowing Your Own Situation 19
   The Role of Credit Bureaus 22
   The Role of Your Business Plan 24
   Working With Your Lender 26
   Not All Assets Are Created Equal! 27
   What Type of Loan do you Need? 32

CHAPTER THREE — GETTING A BUSINESS LOAN 37
   The Most Common Types of Business Loans 39
   The Costs of Getting and Servicing Loans 42
   Borrower Beware: Loan Covenants 49
   Selecting Your Lender 49
   Preparing Your Business Plan 50
   What Interests the Lender 57
   Setting Off Alarms 60
   Presentation 62

CHAPTER FOUR — GETTING A PERSONAL LOAN 65
   Personal Loans 67
   The Most Common Types of Personal Loans 67
   How A Lender Sizes You Up 68
   Tips for Non-W2 Borrowers 75
   Using Mortgage Bankers 75
   What You Can Borrow: Loan Guidelines 77

CONTENTS (continued)

CHAPTER FIVE — PREPARING A SELF-AUDIT TO HELP YOUR LENDER 85
- The Importance of Being Organized 87
- Suggested Organization Plan 87
- The Importance of Self-Auditing: Know Your Weaknesses 89
- Build on Your Strengths 93
- Making an Effective Presentation 94
- Practice Makes Perfect 95

CHAPTER SIX — IF YOU GET TURNED DOWN 97
- What To Do 99
- Are You Using The Right Institution 100
- How to Strengthen Your Hand 104
- How Financial Professionals Can Help 105

CHAPER SEVEN — SBA LOANS 109
- Small Business Administration 111
- The Variety of SBA Loans 111
- Costs of SBA Loans 115
- Two Primary Considerations 118
- SBA Lenders 119
- Typical SBA Requirements 120
- Small Business Investment Companies 121
- Where to Get More Information 122

CHAPTER EIGHT — THE ROLE OF PLANNING 125
- Plan for Success 127
- The Importance of Advance Planning 128
- The Role of Budgeting 132

CONTENTS (continued)

APPENDIXES **135**
   Appendix I — Guideline Review and Checklists for
               Borrowers 137
   Appendix II — Key Documents File 149
   Appendix III — Set Up Your Financial Profile on a
               Spreadsheet 151
   Appendix IV — List of Banks in the SBA CLP/PLP Program ... 165

GLOSSARY **191**

ABOUT THE AUTHOR **197**

CHAPTER ONE

PREPARING FOR THE LENDING PROCESS

A WIDE VARIETY OF LOANS

Applying for credit may be one of the most nerve-wracking things you will ever do, and your success at it can define your future for years to come. To keep your dreams from turning into nightmares, it helps to know as much as you can in advance.

This chapter introduces you to the major concepts in the lending process, such as types of loans and types of lending institutions. We will also cover how to prepare yourself and how to organize your financial data.

We have divided loans into two major groups: personal and business. **Personal loans** are those sought by individuals or families for nonbusiness purposes. Personal loans include:

- Mortgages
- Home equity loans
- Auto and boat financing
- Cash advances on credit cards.

Other common personal loans include:

- Debt consolidation (one large loan used to pay off many smaller ones such as credit cards)
- Assistance with medical or education expenses.

Business loans typically are more involved, because a business cannot simply submit a W2 form and pay stub to prove its income. A business needs to provide a more detailed breakdown of how the loan will be repaid. This is done through preparation of a "pro forma" financial statement projection for the business over the next five years.

Most people probably think of business loans primarily as getting money to finance a new or a start-up operation. However, a business may need a loan for many common reasons, including:

- Expansion (e.g., of the physical plant or into new marketing areas)
- Buying new equipment
- Financing a cash flow gap between your accounts receivable and accounts payable
- Buying out partners or competitors.

Loans to finance new businesses are difficult to get, because lenders have very little experience to go on when evaluating the business.

The Tax Reform Act of 1986 dramatically changed many aspects of tax planning for both individuals and businesses.

Interest incurred on business loans is still fully tax deductible in most cases. Consult a CPA or other tax specialist before making any major financial changes to take advantage of the continued deductibility of business interest.

Lenders do not expect to help finance all aspects of your business. They want to see evidence of capital infusions from investors, including but not necessarily limited to the business' owners. If your business is profitable, with good growth potential, then you or investors you locate should be willing to invest with the prospect of participating in the growth.

If you are turned down for conventional funding for your business, ask if that lender has an equity financing or venture capital department that may be interested.

A WIDE VARIETY OF LENDERS

Banks

Although it is common to think of loans as originating with "banks," there are two quite different types of banks. Most people are more familiar with retail banks. They feature convenient branch offices and offer services typically associated with banking such as savings accounts, safe deposit boxes, checking accounts, credit cards and other common services. They tend to be authorized to lend relatively small amounts, usually for things such as autos, boats or other installment loans. This type of bank plays a major role in the financial lives of people in rural communities. Often loans are approved based on personal relationships rather than objective criteria.

Commercial banks, on the other hand, are oriented toward providing businesses with the services such as cash management and accounts receivable funding that they need. They handle business loans and emphasize long-term business relationships.

Savings & Loan Associations (S&Ls) and Finance Companies

S&Ls were originally conceived as associations of like-minded savers, in specific geographical areas, which were organized to provide money for mortgage loans. Until the deregulation of the financial markets in the 1980s, real estate lending was almost their sole business.

While many S&Ls now do offer loans other than real estate, not all had the experience to handle these loans properly. The 1980s saw many S&L failures.

Finance companies are organizations of investors who seek to lend their own or investors' money (rather than depositors' money). Typically, finance companies' interest rates are very high even for secured loans.

Since they do not lend depositors' money, finance companies are not as tightly regulated. They are not subject to the same usury laws as other lenders. For example, Washington state banks can charge up to 18% interest, while a finance company can charge up to 36%.

Don't be fooled by the interest rate alone. Fees charged to process the loan can raise the real interest rate substantially. Finance companies should usually be considered your last resort because of their normally higher costs.

Loan Intermediaries

Using a mortgage broker can often save you time and aggravation because they know how to prepare your loan request and what local institutions require. Their "insider" knowledge can help you more readily qualify for the loan.

Mortgage brokers make their money from fees on loans. Some **brokers are more interested in their fees than in your business concerns.** Check out any broker's recommendations with your CPA or an attorney before acting.

There are other "loan merchants" who will help you put together a loan proposal and help you find a lender. One good example of this type of broker would be a certified development company (CDC), which is licensed by the Small Business Administration (SBA) to prepare SBA loan proposals.

Alternative Sources of Money

Another source of money is the "hard-money lender." Say you have purchased a new house contingent upon the sale of your current home. If your current home does not sell within the allotted time, a hard-money lender lends you the difference needed to buy the second home, secured by the cash from the ultimate sale of your first home.

The costs of borrowing from hard-money lenders are usually steep. Following this route, you wind up paying three mortgages (the new house, your current house and the hard-money lender's loan) until the sale of your first home.

Venture capitalists lend money to start-up companies for part ownership. Many entrepreneurs have soured on venture capitalists because of the high price involved. In addition, most venture capitalist companies are not interested in small start-ups. They usually require that you give up controlling interest to get their participation. If you have a dispute in the future, they can force you out of your own company!

According to the SBA, the largest source of investment capital for small businesses is from informal sources. These sources are **"angels"**: family members, friends or business associates. They won't be located through the Yellow Pages but rather through your personal contacts. And we are not talking small potatoes here. The SBA estimates that angels invest over $50 billion a year in small businesses.

Points to Remember

1. Banks are not interested in loaning you all the money you will need in your business venture. You need to invest your own capital or find investors.

2. There are many types of lenders.

3. Be sure you are talking to the right institution for the loan you need.

4. Experienced loan brokers can save you time, trouble and even money by matching your specific needs with the right lender.

5. Small businesses often get their financing from informal financing angels.

THE KEY IS PREPARATION

Many entrepreneurs who understand the great effort it takes to be successful will approach getting a loan almost as an afterthought. The two main considerations borrowers must face when applying for a loan are whether they can get the loan, and the cost of getting the loan.

While the first may be your primary concern, sometimes the cost of a loan outweighs any economic value it may hold for you. The more risk lenders perceive, the higher the interest rate they will charge.

Banks no longer refer to their prime rate. "Cost of funds" is a common alternative, which is the interest rate that banks (theoretically at least) charge to their most creditworthy business customers. Most businesses end up paying "prime plus" (an amount over the prime rate). The less stable or creditworthy a business is considered, the higher the rate.

What You Have

Your assets or the things you own (e.g., cash, car, boat, equity in your home, stocks, bonds, business interests), are of interest to a lender. Your assets are those Not all assets are created equal! Lenders prefer certain types of assets over others. For example, if you are seeking a business loan that will be secured by your company's equipment, a lender will look more favorably on large saleable items such as a truck or bulldozer than on things such a sprinkler pipe or specialized software.

Your income, in the case of a personal loan, or your company's cash flow, in the case of a business loan, are of paramount concern for any lender. It is not enough simply to have assets.

EXAMPLE

A widow with no income and her sole asset being a $1 million dollar house will have a difficult time getting a conventional loan, regardless of the value of the home, because there is no income to cover the payments.

Banks are in the banking business, not the real estate business. They want to make their income on interest charged, not the foreclosure or sale of your home.

The amount of your income or cash flow is not the only consideration for a lender.

- ▶ How long have you earned money at your current level?
- ▶ How long is your business' track record?
- ▶ How stable is that income or cash flow? If you earned $60,000 in the current year but only $25,000 in the two previous years, you will need to show why your lender should base its decision on the higher level. In the case of a business, your profit history is vital information.
- ▶ Do your costs stay under control as your sales grow?
- ▶ Are your costs affected by seasonal considerations? If so, what provisions have you made to smooth out the fluctuations?

Lenders are interested in your profit growth, not sales increases. Strongly increasing sales means nothing if costs are rising even faster. Lenders want to see that sales growth is accompanied by cost increases that rise slower or at least no faster than the sales. They look for rising profitability, not only sales.

You also have other assets. Some may be tangible, while others, such as your education or experience, are intangible but nonetheless valuable.

- ▶ Do you know what type of loan you need?
- ▶ Do you know what type of lender you need?
- ▶ Do you know how to prepare to get your loan?
- ▶ Are you organized?

Your Turn

Which of the following would you consider your tangible and intangible assets?

Tangible   Intangible

_____   _____

_____   _____

_____   _____

- ▶ Do you have 10 or 15 years' experience in the field?
- ▶ Do you have an MBA from a prestigious school?
- ▶ Has your income progressed steadily in your career?
- ▶ Is there good reason to expect further increases? Have you exhibited stability in your professional career?
- ▶ Is your business a venture that a lender will understand and get excited about?
- ▶ Do you, your partners, or your executives have special qualifications for your business (e.g., have they been in similar capacities in successful ventures in the past)?
- ▶ Is there something unique to your business (e.g., cost or innovation advantage)?

What You Need

It is important that you establish your needs in a logical, sensible manner. For example, if you plan to buy a house that is listed for $250,000, you should be sure that you are paying fair market value. Check out previous selling prices of similar properties in the area, or have an appraisal done if there is any doubt.

Lenders base the amount they will lend on the appraised value or what you paid, whichever is lower. Overpaying for a piece of property because of anxiousness or susceptibility to an agent's sales pitch doesn't reflect well on your investment acumen. If you have some inside knowledge of a particular business situation that justifies paying more than the amount of a lender's appraisal, you should explain it to your lender. However, you will need to show that you can afford the higher price because the lender will normally loan only 66% to 80% of the appraised value, 90% for some housing with mortgage insurance.

In the case of a business loan for expansion, you will need to research the matter thoroughly. Establish the production costs exactly, assessing if there will be additional marketing costs and asking what the payment history of your account receivables is. (This is a major consideration in substantiating your cash flow.)

Also know what additional sales you can reasonably expect. Why are these projections reasonable? Do you have independent expert opinions on your profit figures? Do the profit figures justify the expansion and the loan? If it doesn't make economic sense, no lender will extend a loan.

In recent years, some financial advisors have suggested that it makes good sense to use 15-year mortgages instead of the more traditional 30-year loans. In most cases, we suggest staying with a 30-year term (for the added flexibility) with a no prepayment penalty clause.

Types of personal and business loans can vary. One kind of business loan is called an **annual line of credit**, which can have different term arrangements. Another kind of business loan is a **revolving line of credit**, which is much like a credit card. Each time you pay off part of the principal of the loan, your line of credit is replenished by a set amount. A **term loan** has a fixed time period and fixed rate amount to be repaid on a given date.

With a term loan, as you pay off the loan you lower your total debt load, but do not renew your credit. You will need to reapply to get additional credit. You can structure loan terms in a variety of ways. For example, in a business you may need cash in the short term, but later when cash flow has picked up, you will have plenty. A term loan with a balloon payment may work best. This means that you would pay small regular payments and one large final payment (the balloon payment).

Understanding loan options, including balloon or interest-only loans, and knowing what you can afford will go a long way toward coming to an agreement with your lender.

When you are working on your financing figures, be conservative. Don't be afraid to provide for a cash reserve for your business. Lenders like to see a conservative posture. What they most dread is having the loan go sour. Lenders know that no one knows the future with certainty. Those who are experienced with business loans realize that most businesses go through cycles.

What Lenders Require

Lenders require that you supply certain documents which they use for very specific reasons. By comparing the data revealed on each of these documents, they get a feeling not only of what you can afford but how honest you are with them. For example, if you inflate the value of your car by putting its list price as its value, they have reason to suspect the rest of your figures. Cars depreciate 20% to 30% as soon as you drive them off the showroom floor.

For a personal loan, you will complete a detailed application. Depending on the size of the loan, you may be asked to provide copies of your W2 form showing your current income. Be prepared also with a current pay stub. Often you will be asked to provide copies of your last two or three tax returns.

If you are asking for a sizeable loan, or if you are not a W2 employee, you will probably also be asked to prepare a balance sheet and an income statement or a cash flow statement. A **balance sheet** is an accounting of your assets and your liabilities. Your net worth is the difference between them. An **income statement** is an accounting of your income and expenses. It itemizes your sources of income and your expenses. A **cash flow statement** details your cash inflows and outflows. Many financial planners and planning books confuse these two. CPAs and bankers, though, do make a clear distinction.

When you itemize your expenses, you generally list your mortgage and car payments as an expense. However, technically, only the amount of each of those payments that goes to pay the interest due is an expense. The balance builds your equity in the respective asset (i.e., the difference between an income statement and a cash flow statement).

Lenders want to see what asset building you are doing, of course, but they are primarily interested in whether your cash flow is sufficient to cover the payments you are obligated to make. A cash flow statement reveals how much money you have on hand after paying for necessary expenses such as housing, clothing, food, utilities, transportation and other debt service. The distinction between income and cash flow statements may seem overly technical. However, you want to be sure you are speaking your lender's language. They are interested mainly in your cash flow picture. In most cases when applying for a business loan, you will be asked to provide all of the items below.

- ► Loan application
- ► Tax returns

- Balance sheet
- Income and cash flow statements
- A detailed business plan.

Your business plan is a critical part of getting the loan. The plan must include a discussion of your company. What is it that you do? Make sure the lender understands your business. Remember, the safest answer for lenders is no. You need to convince them why yes is the right answer for you.

In addition to describing the business, you need to detail the qualifications of your important people. Lenders look to see that a business is run by executives with appropriate credentials. Do they have management or finance experience? Who is in charge of marketing?

Your business plan must describe why you want the loan. Include cash flow projections for the next five years. (Lenders realize that beyond that the figures become very speculative.) Your lender wants to see net cash flow (after expenses) broken down by month for the first 24 months and by quarter for the following 36 months.

Most requests for business loans are rejected because owners fail to communicate effectively what the business is and what they are planning. The business plan plays a crucial role in the ultimate success of getting a loan for your business, because it explains what your business does, why it is successful at what it does and how and when the lender will get repaid for the loan.

Points to Remember

1. Approach getting a loan with the same diligence and thoroughness you use in all business planning.

2. The cost of a loan will be in proportion to the perceived risk for the lender.

3. Liquid marketable assets are valued more by lenders than specialized items.

4. Lenders look first at level and stability of income and cash flow.

5. Know precisely how much you need and why.

6. Structure a loan to fit your cash flow needs.

7. Be prepared to submit two years' tax returns, a current balance sheet, income and cash flow statements, a loan application and, for a business, a business plan.

8. A carefully written and detailed business plan that is presented well will make the difference between getting a loan and being turned down.

ADVANCE PLANNING CAN MAKE THE DIFFERENCE

When you are seeking a loan, you must make use of your understanding of the total picture.

For example, if you plan to go into business in the future, start it now and take out the loans you need while you are still a wage earner. Banks and other lenders do not like to fund new businesses, and are more likely to fund someone with a steady income. They see more than 80% of new businesses fail within three years.

You are a much better credit risk than a new, unproven business:

▶ If you have a good credit record

▶ If you have earned a good income for three to five years

▶ If you have accumulated reasonable assets.

If your sole income will be derived from this new business, your lender will be leery of your ability to sustain sufficient income to cover the loan payments, because the business has no track record. A change in careers will set off alarms for a lender. Remember, bankers want to see evidence of stability.

Advance planning also requires that you have a firm understanding of your financial situation. When you apply for a loan, it is essential that you know the exact amount you need. If you underestimate and then have to go back to your lender to request additional money, you start off on a poor footing. Your lender relied on your numbers in approving the first loan. Now you come back to say that you were wrong. Get enough the first time.

The Importance of Being Organized

To create a good impression with a lender, you need to organize your presentation. The more complex your situation, the more difficult it is to know all the facts off the top of your head. Use a written agenda when discussing your loan request.

Lenders want stability. If you plan a significant change in your life, it may be best to apply for any loans before making the change. A key first step to making a favorable impression on prospective lenders is being organized. Know where to find any information they may need.

Appendix I includes a basic balance sheet and income statement, worksheets for determining appropriate financial ratios that lenders use and a worksheet for comparing adjustable and fixed-rate loans. These will help you in organizing your presentation. In addition, the loan preparation checklists in Appendix I will assist you in putting your information into a logical order so you can quickly find any data you may need.

ASK YOURSELF

- ▶ What type of loan do you need? Why?
- ▶ What type of lender do you need? Why?
- ▶ What preparation will you need to do to get your loan?

CHAPTER TWO

ORGANIZING YOUR LOAN PROPOSAL

KNOWING YOUR OWN SITUATION

This chapter describes the necessary steps that must be taken to give you a realistic idea of your loan needs. To succeed in processing a loan, you must first determine exactly where you stand financially. If you want a business loan, you need to generate cash flow projections as part of your business plan. This chapter will guide you in that process. In addition, we will show you how to select and what to expect from your lender.

Conducting a "self-audit" before meeting with a lender is an important part of being prepared. A major reason people get turned down on loan applications is their failure to understand their financial situation. For many people, the reluctance to take the time to sort out their finances is due to a vague uneasiness about what they will discover. The lenders will make a diligent effort to uncover all the details of your financial condition.

Your Balance Sheet

A balance sheet is simply an accounting of your assets (the things you own) and your liabilities (what you owe). The bottom line of a balance sheet is your net worth, your assets minus your liabilities.

Page 20 shows an asset worksheet. If your liabilities are greater than your assets, you have a negative net worth. If you find that you do have a negative or negligible net worth, you can improve the picture by reducing your liabilities or increasing your assets.

Notes receivable would be loans you have made to friends or business associates. If you have an outstanding note, be sure to include the balance due you with covenants and terms of payment.

Asset Worksheet

1.	Checking Accounts, Savings Accounts, Money Market Funds.	$
2.	Certificates of Deposit (C.D.s), Stocks, Bonds, T-Bills, Notes Receivable, Mutual Funds (that mature or are sellable within 12 months).	$
3.	Limited Partnerships, Annuities, etc., that could be sold within 12 months.	$
4.	Home, Rental Property, 2nd Home Raw land.	$
5.	The amount you would receive if you cashed in your whole or universal life insurance policy. (Term life insurance has a cash value of zero.)	$
6.	CD's, Stocks, Bonds, T-Bills, Notes Receivable, that will mature after 12 months.	$
7.	IRAs, 401(K)s, Keoghs, Employee-Provided Retirement Plans.	$
8.	Limited Partnerships and Annuities that would be sold after 12 months; the value of small businesses, cars, boats, jewelry, art, household furnishings and collectables.	$
9.	Amounts you owe others in the next 12 months. Notes Payable, Credit Lines, amounts due on any investments and taxes due.	$
10.	Amounts you owe others for your Real Estate (home) in the next 12 months.	$
11.	Amount owing on all credit cards.	$
12.	Car and boat loans due in the next 12 months.	$
13.	Amounts you owe others, less the amount reported in 9 Notes Payable Current.	$
14.	Amounts you owe others for Real Estate (home), less the amount reported in 10 Mortgages Current.	$
15.	Car and boat loans due, less the amount reported in 12 other Current Liabilities.	$
16.	Any other future contractual commitment to pay (net reported above) such as a balloon payment in 2 years.	$
	A. Add lines 1, 2 and 3	$
	B. Add lines A, 4, 5, 6, 7 and 8	$
	C. Add lines 9, 10, 11 and 12	$
	D. Add lines C, 13, 14, 15 and 16	$
	E. Subtract line D from line B	$
	F. Add lines D and E CAUTION: Line B and F must be the same.	$
17.	Salary, Bonus, Honorariums and 1099 Income Royalties.	$
18.	Net income from properties you own and rent.	$
19.	Dividends from stocks.	$
20.	Interest from Savings Accounts, Money Markets, C.D.s, Bonds, etc.	$
21.	Alimony, Child Support, Social Security.	$
22.	House payment or rent you pay on any Real Estate you own.	$
23.	Federal and State income taxes, sales taxes, Social Security, car license, property taxes, etc.	$
24.	Interest expense for all loans and credit card balances you have outstanding.	$
25.	Food, clothing, household expenses, transportation, insurance.	$
26.	Medical, education, recreation and entertainment.	$
	G. Add lines 17, 18, 19, 20 and 21.	$
	H. Add lines 22, 23, 24, 25 and 26.	$
	I. Subtract H from G.	$

Use professional appraisers' newspaper ads and open houses in your neighborhood to determine value. A local real estate agent should be able to give you a good idea of your home's market value. Many loan application and balance sheet forms lump personal property into one line. However, we have found that by breaking your personal property holdings down into a few classes, you can identify some assets that a lender will find more palatable as potential collateral.

A common mistake is to overvalue one's car. Your lender can quickly check what the market value of your car in the *Kelly Blue Book* or simply by looking in the classified ads in the newspaper. If you own valuable collectibles such as rare coins, stamps or art, get them appraised by a third party.

Since jewelry and furs are more marketable than, say, furniture, show these separately. Remember to list market or depreciated values. Neither the lender nor a potential buyer cares what you paid for the items.

If you significantly undervalue the amount of your credit card's outstanding balances, it will show up on a credit report. That will hurt your credibility with the lender.

One way to determine expenses is to look over your check register for the past few months to get a good idea of monthly expenses.

The value of small businesses is difficult to assess in most cases. If you are the sole owner of a small business, you will need to determine the value of its tangible assets minus liabilities.

An established business with a base of customers is also entitled to some value over and above the specific assets. This is called "goodwill." Consult your CPA or an investment banker for a realistic estimate. Remember, you may have to justify any figures here to the lender.

1. Does your balance sheet detail your assets, liabilities and net worth?
2. Does your income statement itemize your income and expenses?
3. Does your cash flow statement itemize your cash inflows and outflows?
4. Do you understand your exact financial situation before applying for a loan?

THE ROLE OF CREDIT BUREAUS

Good credit, once lost, can never be regained. Every lender will want to check your credit record. Lenders will obtain copies of credit reports on you—your credit history—from one or more credit bureaus, which are clearinghouses for information on consumers' credit histories. The five major credit bureaus are Trans Union, Chilton, CBI, Associated Credit Services and TRW, although 2,000 operate nationally.

Lenders subscribe to one or more credit services. As part of their subscription, they provide the bureaus with information on their borrowers. This information from lenders makes up your credit report.

Obtain a copy of your credit report before applying for any loan; you should review your credit history every two to three years. TRW provides a regular subscription service to help you keep tabs on your credit record. Called "TRW Credentials," this service, for a fee, entitles you to get a copy of your TRW credit report as often as you want. In addition, you receive automatic notification when anyone gets a copy of your credit report. For more information, call (800) 262-7432 or write TRW Credentials Service, P.O. Box 2132, Chatsworth, CA 91313.

Most credit bureaus will sell you a copy of your report. Typical charges range from $8 to $15 for a single report. You must provide your Social Security number, signature, telephone number and usually your address for the past three years.

You are entitled to receive at no charge a copy of any credit report that is used by a lender when you are denied credit. Federal law requires lenders to tell you what reports they relied on.

A credit report contains your:

- ► Current address
- ► Previous addresses
- ► Social Security number
- ► Marital status
- ► Number of dependents
- ► Past and present employment data, including salary history
- ► How many credit cards you have
- ► What credit line each has
- ► Whether you have any late payments
- ► How many late payments
- ► Current balances
- ► Serious credit problems such as loans sent to collection services
- ► Any public records such as bankruptcy tax liens, foreclosures, civil suits and judgments or other legal proceedings such as criminal convictions
- ► The frequency and names of institutions that have requested your report

If there are errors in the report, you should put your complaints in writing and send them to the bureau in question. The law requires the bureaus to investigate and delete data that can't be verified. If the bureau insists there is no mistake and you can't track down the information to correct it, all is not lost. *You are entitled to include a 100-word explanatory note to your file that must go out with every report.*

Credit reports are a major factor in lenders' decisions. Once they have gone through your documents and scored the application according to their internal checklists, they use credit reports to confirm whether the information you provide regarding your debt load and income is accurate. The correlation between the two is critical in determining the lenders' evaluation of subjective elements such as your credibility. That is why you should be conservative, up front, and honest about both the positives and the negatives to your story.

Once a lender has turned up some negative information that you failed to mention, your explanations will have less impact than if you had mentioned it before. Remember: Lenders have access to independent verification of much of your credit history through credit bureaus. You should obtain a copy of your credit report before applying for a loan. Your credit report contains details of how much credit you now have as well as how well you have paid debts in the past.

THE ROLE OF YOUR BUSINESS PLAN

Business loans are more subjective than personal loans. A credit report won't tell a lender anything about the future prospects for your company. You must ensure credibility in your business plan. Simple statements don't carry much weight. Provide evidence in support of your opinions.

Cite authorities (e.g., from magazine, newspaper, newsletter articles) who agree with you. Acquaint the lender with your market and its trends. Explain why you are in a good position to take advantage of those trends. The bigger the loan, the more important it is that the lender understand your business.

Your CPA or attorney may be able to explain things in the lender's own terms. It is important to have your CPA take an active part in developing one of the most important parts of your business plan: the cash flow projections for the next five years. Even if the figures would be the same with you doing the numbers yourself, it's better to hire a CPA. The presence of a CPA adds credibility to the figures. You want to do everything possible to make sure the lender is comfortable with those numbers.

Business Uncertainties

It is important to show the lender that you have made provisions for future changes both personally and for the business. Lenders often don't ask about provisions for key employees becoming disabled, for instance.

It is a sign of thorough planning if you show that you have implemented a disability plan. Explain contingency plans in case you become disabled yourself. You should have insurance coverage sufficient to repay the loan in case you die or become disabled. This is especially important if your business is a one- or two-person operation that would have a difficult time earning its income without your full participation.

Have a durable power of attorney for running the business if you become disabled. Prepare a will that stipulates who will take over and run your business immediately in case of your death. Make sure your lender knows who the executor of that will is.

If you have partners in your business (whether a partnership or a closely held corporation), have an attorney draw up a buy/sell agreement among the principals. The agreement should include a method for valuing the business. It should also define how the partners can sell it themselves in case anything goes wrong with the loan at a later date. They need to show that they did their job.

Sometimes success in procuring a loan is merely the result of presenting the same facts but in such as way as to achieve the qualifying score you need. Lenders look for four main elements:

1. Ability to repay loan
2. History of timely payment of debts
3. Quality assets in case the loan fails
4. A secondary source of repayment
    - ▶ Lenders use a scoring system based on their previous experiences with different types of borrowers. Lenders carefully review all documents submitted for consistency. Inconsistencies will trigger alarms. For example:

- Does your interest income correspond with bank balances?
- Does your dividend income correspond with stock holdings?
- Do your interest expense tax deductions correspond with listed debts?
- Does your claimed income correspond with what is reported on your tax returns?

WORKING WITH YOUR LENDER

The most desirable situation is to establish a good rapport with your lender. Don't take your lender for granted! Usually borrowers are very careful to tiptoe through the lending process until a loan is approved. After that, it's as though they don't remember the loan officer or the institution itself except as the destiny of the monthly loan payment.

Borrowing is not usually a one shot deal. Once you have purchased your home, you may want to remodel it. You may have children who will need money for education. An entrepreneur who borrows to buy new equipment may want to expand the business at a later date. Other replacement equipment may be needed. Helping to finance a cash flow gap between accounts receivable and accounts payable is a common need.

Understand the importance of the overall banking relationship.

EXAMPLE

Your company has a $100,000 one-year CD, paying 7.5 percent with Central Bank, where you also have a $250,000 line of credit loan. You are tempted to move your CD to Outback Bank where one-year CD rates are 8.5 percent. Even if there are no restrictive clauses in your lending arrangements, be assured that Central Bank is aware of your deposits and other business transacted with them. While it may seem advantageous to earn a higher rate at another bank, when it comes time for renewal of your loan with Central, you are likely to pay a higher interest rate.

It is important that you keep your banker apprised of significant developments. If your frozen yogurt business experiences an unexpected sales slowdown due to unseasonably cool temperatures, resulting in a late monthly payment or inability to meet the monthly payment, call your bank officer ahead of time and explain the problem. Don't get in a situation of having to explain any problems after the fact. If lenders realize that you won't hide adverse developments from them, they will feel more comfortable helping you over the inevitable down cycles that every business experiences.

Don't limit your contact with lenders to problems. Share good news and your future plans with them. Keep them apprised of future prospects. Make them feel they are part of the team.

NOT ALL ASSETS ARE CREATED EQUAL!

Having a large net worth is no guarantee of getting a loan. Primary among many other considerations is that you or your business have sufficient cash flow to cover the loan payments. But even if you have a good income and a good track record in paying your debts, lenders still want to see what type of assets you have accumulated.

Potential Problems with Real Estate

Not all assets are created equal. Some assets may look good to you on your balance sheet but will trigger alarms for lenders rather than create any sense of security. One asset that cuts both ways is nonincome producing property.

EXAMPLE

Inner-City Realty owns an apartment house where occupancy rates have been low and where deteriorating conditions will require substantial investment for improvement. A lender may shy away from loaning the company money for other purposes because the property may become a drain on its cash flow. The lender realizes that if occupancy rates drop, cash flow may be squeezed too tight to cover the loan. The owner must be prepared to show why that won't happen, or what provisions have been made for that eventuality.

If you own leveraged farm property or equipment and have borrowed to finance the property, a lender may be concerned. Farming is very cyclical. In down cycles, the burden of heavy debt incurred buying land or equipment can cause large drains on cash flow.

Even when considering your own home as an asset, keep in mind that lenders may look at things differently than you do. For example, that new swimming pool you added last year may not augment the value of your house as much as you expected. Lenders know that it costs an average of $300 per month to maintain a swimming pool. Don't be surprised if your net income is reduced by that amount for the lender's calculations. A lower cash flow means you qualify for a smaller loan.

While we tend to consider higher-priced homes as signs of success, at some point your lender will discount some of that when figuring its repossession value. Also, very high-priced specialized home (which includes unique features that you wanted but are not necessarily things most home buyers seek) is harder to sell. Unless you sign over a first deed of trust on your home, a lender knows that at least part of your equity in the home will be protected by a bankruptcy court.

If your business is involved with toxins or chemicals, even its real estate value (which many people think is virtually invulnerable to severe price drops) may be impaired.

EXAMPLE

If your gas station were to close, the land will not be as valuable as surrounding property because of the potentially high cost of state or federal mandated cleanup before the land could be used for other purposes.

Liability laws in this area pose real problems to land owners. The courts have held that all owners of a piece of land after it has been contaminated by toxins may be liable for future costs and damage. In other words, even if you did not realize that the property you bought from Joe Conman was environmentally damaged when you sold it to another party, that party may have a claim against you later.

Problem Investments

Other assets that may concern your lender include outdated technologies. If your business is a manufacturing concern, a lender will realize that outmoded equipment hurts competitiveness.

If you are an investor in a partnership with liability for future capital calls, your income or cash flow projections will be discounted by the lender. Partnership interests are notoriously illiquid. Plan on your lender discounting net asset value estimates.

Ask for enough money the first time. Don't get in a situation of having to go back for more money. For example, if you have potential exposure for a $200,000 capital call from an investment, don't ask for a line of credit for $100,000 because you don't think the partnership could possibly ever need more. If all other things are acceptable (cash flow, stability, assets) and you have the $200,000 exposure, ask for $200,000. The lender will be more comfortable knowing that you will have enough money to cover potential liabilities and he/she won't be put in the position of having to approve another loan to protect the first one.

If you own stock in a closely held company, it is virtually unmarketable. Letter stock or "144 stock" cannot be easily sold. It won't do your lender any good to seize something for a delinquent loan that can't be used to reduce your indebtedness. Expect a discounted value.

The valuation of personal businesses is a very tricky area. While your valuation may be perfectly legitimate for a going concern, it does not reflect what could be obtained if you were no longer running the company or if you were to sell it at a distressed price. If something developed that hurt your business so that you could no longer generate sufficient cash flow to repay the loan, then it would no longer be as valuable. About the only thing a lender could then sell would be tangible assets, which would be used and depreciated.

In addition, certain prepaid assets hold little collateral value for a lender because they would not be worth much in liquidation. For example, if you prepay your rent or insurance premiums to get a discount, that is an asset to your company. However, it interests a lender only as it affects your cash flow, not as collateral. Deposits that you have paid for things such as equipment leases, rent or utilities are also of negligible value.

Problem Personal Assets

Personal loan applications have a line for estimating the value of your household goods. While your furniture may seem valuable to you for many reasons, a lender will value it at about 10 cents on the dollar of the purchase price.

Attach a note to your financial statements saying that artwork and other collectibles are listed at retail value. If you have current appraisals, include them. If not, note how you arrived at the value (e.g., questioned local art gallery). Artwork and collectibles will be valued by the lender at wholesale value, or approximately 50 cents on the dollar, which is what a lender could sell it for quickly.

Your Turn

Answer the following questions:

1. Which of your assets present liquidation problems?
2. Assess their value, taking into consideration the lender's discount.

"I just want to have some money available in case something happens." This will immediately create suspicion that perhaps things are not as you reported.

Legitimate business purposes include such things as:

- Expansion
- Financing operations (e.g., smoothing out cash flow between your billings and receipt of money)
- Employee training
- New equipment

Legitimate personal purposes included such things as:

- New car
- New home
- New recreation vehicle
- Children's education
- Debt consolidation
- Home remodeling

Know exactly what it is you need. For example, supply the lender with written material describing new equipment. Tell them why you need it. Explain what it will do to enhance your business and increase your net profit (e.g., reduce your costs).

Items with a good liquidation value that will improve the bottom line, such as equipment, are likely to get a more sympathetic ear. Things like training will need to be explained in some detail. Stress the specific bottom-line benefits that the training will produce. If your business entails a considerable amount of correspondence with customers, show how training in the use of a word processor designed for that purpose will reduce expense or enhance productivity and increase profitability.

Personal Loans

In most cases in applying for a personal loan, you will know the exact cost of the items.

Keep in mind that a lender will extend a loan based only on the appraised value of a house, not on what you agreed to pay for it.

For some personal loans, the lender retains title in the item until the loan is paid in full. For example: When you buy a car it may be registered in your name, but the legal owner is the lender. With a mortgage loan you legally own the house, but the mortgagor has a deed of trust (lien) on the property. The lien holder is clearly identified on the title.

Lenders tend not to make a mortgage loan for more than the purchase price, even if the appraisal value is more. They will loan only 66 percent to 80 percent of the purchase price.

► Know exactly how much money you need and why.

► For a business loan, explain why the loan will benefit the company in financial terms.

WHAT TYPE OF LOAN DO YOU NEED?

Secured Vs. Unsecured

Loans can be secured or unsecured. When we refer to secured loans, we mean loans for which specific collateral has been pledged. For a mortgage loan, the collateral is the first deed of trust on the house. For a car loan, it is the title to the automobile.

There are many different types of secured loans. You may be able to get more favorable rates if you secure the loan with specific items.

EXAMPLE:

Your business is selling equipment to other businesses, but you need money first to buy the equipment. You go to a lender and pledge the equipment as collateral for a loan. When you are paid by the company where you install the equipment, you pay off the loan and the lender removes any lien.

You may wonder what prevents you as a seller of equipment from pledging the same equipment to two or three banks to get two or three times the amount of money you could get from one lender. When you pledge specific items as collateral, your lender files with the state details of items pledged. This is called a UCC (Uniform Commercial Code) filing. Lenders do check with the state government UCC filings to ensure that you haven't already pledged the collateral to someone else.

Not surprisingly, lenders prefer secured loans. Typically, rates will be less than for unsecured loans of the same amount with comparable terms. Unsecured or "signature" loans are not tied to specific collateral. That does not mean that the lender won't move to seize some valuable assets.

Try to avoid collateralizing your home for business loans. If your business is an established concern, you should be able to get by with a general guarantee (signature). However, if your business is new, you probably will not be able to avoid using your home as collateral.

Terms

Loan terms can be worked out in many ways. A revolving line of credit loan is quite common for businesses. This is a continuous loan where the amount of credit you have is renewed each time you pay down some of the balance. Most business line of credit loan agreements stipulate that there must be a zero balance (no debt outstanding) for at least 30 days each year. In other words, you must pay off any outstanding balance for a continuous 30-day period. This feature distinguishes it from a term loan.

When you take out a line of credit loan that requires a zero balance for 30 days of every year, do not make use of the money for the first 30 days after the loan is approved. Remember, this requires planning. Since you have satisfied the 30-day requirement for the first 12 months, you have 11 months of that year plus the first 11 months of the following year before you have to pay down the balance to zero in the last month of the second year. That gives you 22 months to make full use of the line of credit without worrying about having to pay down the balance.

In the personal sphere most home equity loans are revolving lines of credit. Once you have qualified for a home equity loan of, say, $50,000, you have that amount available on call. When you write a check to use part or all of that money, you begin paying interest at the rate spelled out in the loan papers (typically a formula). When you pay the loan down, your line of credit is replenished for future use if you desire.

Term loans differ from revolving line of credit loans because they have a set length and amount. As you pay off the balance, you do not automatically regain any credit for future use. Once the loan is paid off, you need to reapply for further credit. Mortgage, auto, boat and equipment loans are term loans. Amortization is the process by which you systematically repay your loan. If you take out a 10-year loan, to be repaid in monthly installments, the lender adds in the finance charge and divides the total amount by 120 payments. The longer the loan term, the lower the monthly payments. However, you also know that the longer the term, the more you pay in interest. Even with a term loan, it is possible to vary your repayment schedule.

If you have a short-term cash "crunch," take out a loan amortized over seven years with a balloon payment in year four. Your payments will be lower to help you through the cash crunch and the shorter term (four-year due) will get a better rate. The key is to make certain you will be in a position to make the final (balloon) payment, which will be the balance of the loan. If you cannot, it could burst in your face.

Creative use of balloon payments, a knowledge of how amortization works and a firm understanding of your financial future can be valuable in getting the loan you need with the terms you can afford. Don't be afraid to propose unusual terms to your lender.

Remember

- ▶ Secured loans are generally easier to qualify for and cheaper in cost.
- ▶ A loan can be secured by many kinds of assets, including real estate, equipment, accounts receivable and so on.
- ▶ When an asset is pledged for a loan, your lender will file a UCC report with the state.
- ▶ A line of credit or revolving credit loan replenishes the credit available when the principal is paid down.

▶ Term loans are fixed in length and amount. Once paid off, you must apply again for further credit.

YOUR TURN *Before you turn in an application to a prospective lender, be sure that you have assembled and reviewed the following documents:*

▶ **Personal (use of funds)**

- ☐ Worksheets: balance sheet, income and cash flow statements plus explanatory notes for any unusual items (e.g., auto loan paid off in six months, etc.)
- ☐ Last two or three years' tax returns
- ☐ The lender's applications and requested paperwork, completed and signed
- ☐ W2 and current pay stub

▶ **Business Plan**

- ☐ Purpose, stating amount of loan needed and reason
- ☐ Description of company
- ☐ CPA-prepared financial statements
- ☐ Management team's experience
- ☐ Expert support for projections
- ☐ Cash flow pro formas for five years: on a monthly basis for 24 months, quarterly for the next 36 months (be sure to include repayment of the loan)
- ☐ Your marketing plan
- ☐ Compensation details
- ☐ Company history
- ☐ Unique features of company
- ☐ Corporate or partnership tax returns for the last two or three years
- ☐ Personal tax returns for two years and a personal financial statement
- ☐ Lender application filled out and signed

ASK YOURSELF

- ► Calculate your assets and liabilities and assess your financial situation.
- ► What is the main element to remember when working with your lender?
- ► What is the role of the credit bureau?

CHAPTER THREE

GETTING A BUSINESS LOAN

THE MOST COMMON TYPES OF BUSINESS LOANS

It pays to know about different kinds of loans, because banks have many types to choose from. Ask your loan officer for advice, but understanding the most common kinds of loans will help you pick the correct one.

Line of Credit

A line of credit (LOC) loan is one of the most common types of small business loans. Your lender makes available a fixed sum of money that you can use as the need arises over the term of the loan. The most common term is for one year.

Rates for LOCs run one to three percentage points over the lender's prime rate or cost of funds. You pay interest only on the outstanding balance. Other fees such as a commitment fee or a requirement for a compensating balance (money left on deposit with the lender during the term of the loan) may be charged.

There are different varieties of LOCs. The most common, a *non-binding LOC,* does not guarantee that the full amount of the loan will be available at all times. Many circumstances may result in terminating LOCs, including a change in lending policies by the bank, deterioration in the financial condition of your company, a downturn in the economy (recession), problems in your industry or changes in the regulatory environment for lenders.

If you are willing (and able) to pay more for your loan, you may be able to get a *binding or committed line of credit.* With a binding LOC, you are guaranteed that the money will be available for the full term of the loan.

A *revolving LOC* is similar to a credit card loan. You have a fixed amount available. When you use part of that amount, your credit line is reduced. However, when you pay off the principal, your line is replenished for future use. Usually, a revolving line of credit requires an annual review by the lender.

Most LOCs are secured with accounts receivable (A/R) and/or inventory. Typical loan amounts are 50 to 75 percent of A/R and 50 percent of inventory. An established company with a good track record may qualify for more depending on the lender's in-house requirements.

EXAMPLE

Gerri Built Construction company gets the construction contract for a new office building. Since Mr. Built is paid in installments as the project is completed, he needs initial funding for materials, workers and overhead. He makes an arrangement with a lender for a LOC to cover his continuous expenses. He assigns the installment payments he would receive from the developer directly to the lender. His A/R collateralized his loan.

EXAMPLE

Wheeler Dealer is in the used car business. Since a car dealer needs inventory to be successful, Wheeler goes to his banker for an LOC loan. The bank wants security for the loan. They agree on the following terms: He turns over the pink slip (legal title) to his bank when he buys a car with his line of credit. When he sells the car, he pays down his LOC, and the bank gives him back the pink slip so he can transfer title to the new car owner.

Factoring

Factoring is another term for accounts receivable financing.

If your growing company needs its cash flow more quickly, you can work out an arrangement to be paid immediately. Naturally this option will cost more because the lender (or "factor") has higher costs (the cost of the money advanced) and higher risk.

Factoring entails a lender buying your accounts receivable as they occur. It works this way: When you receive an order, you submit the details to your lender. If the lender approves, you are advanced a discounted amount (e.g., 65 to 85 percent) for the order. The lender then assumes responsibility for collecting on the A/R.

As you might suspect, this type of financing is considerably more expensive than a LOC secured by your A/Rs because the lender assumes all the risk and costs of collection. A factoring system can be set up in many different ways. For example, you may work with your lender to establish credit limits and average collection times for each of your customers. You send copies of invoices directly to the lender. You get paid minus the lender's fees at the agreed-upon time period.

EXAMPLE

Bill Denim owns an apparel manufacturing company. His growing company requires ready cash to finance expanding sales efforts. Also, he wants to save the money that a credit department would cost. He prefers to use the money for marketing. He enters a factoring agreement with a local lender. Copies of his customer invoices are sent directly to his lender. The lender makes immediate (though discounted) payment to Bill's company. The lender now owns the A/R and will collect from Bill's customers. Bill's responsibility and concern over payment is ended. He can concentrate his time on other aspects of his business.

Term Loans

Business term loans are for a set amount and time period. They range from one year to 15 years, but most are for one to seven years. They are used for a variety of purposes:

- ▶ Bridging a working capital gap
- ▶ Expansion
- ▶ Buying equipment
- ▶ Paying off other debt (such as a balloon payment).

Usually lenders require some type of collateral on a term loan. Just as with LOC loans, term loans can be secured with accounts receivable or inventory. Another common approach is to use a company's fixed assets. The most acceptable type of assets are things like manufacturing machinery, trucks, tractors or other heavy equipment. Assets that are specific to your business have less value, making financing difficult to obtain.

EXAMPLE

If you had computer software specially written for your business, it may be of great value to you, but of little interest to a lender as collateral.

Your lender will require appraisals. The two most common methods are fair market value and replacement value. Fair market value is usually the highest value since it assumes no time or economic constraints for its sale. Replacement value is the estimate of what it would cost to replace the asset with a similar product (age and purpose).

It is possible to make a loan more attractive to your lender and less costly to you at the same time. Assume that a seven-year loan is the length you need to get the smaller monthly payments you can afford. Say that loan carries a 14 percent rate. Your projections show that your financial condition will be much stronger in three years.

Try this: ask for a seven-year amortization schedule for your loan, but with a balloon payment for the balance due in three years. Since the lender's risk for a three-year loan is less than for a seven-year loan, you may be able to get the loan at 12 percent or 13 percent. At the same time, you have the lower monthly payments you require and three years to make the balloon payment or arrange financing. Plan ahead to make sure you can arrange to make the balloon payment.

Your Turn

Answer the following questions:

1. What are the common types of business loans?
2. Is a nonbinding line of credit loan subject to termination at the lender's discretion?
3. Does a revolving line of credit replenish your credit as principal payments are made?
4. What is common security for business loans?

THE COSTS OF GETTING AND SERVICING LOANS

When you take out a loan you will pay finance charges, interest and "carrying costs" (the costs the lender incurs such as bookkeeping, collection and insurance). You may be familiar with carrying costs if you have ever had a mortgage or a home equity loan. Usually with these types of loans you paid "points" to get the loan. Another type of carrying cost is the annual fee that many credit cards charge.

The most common method of assessing interest is add-on interest. Finance charges are simply added to the principal amount borrowed. For example, if a lender agrees to loan you $2,000 with a finance charge of $200, that $200 will be added to the principal amount. You receive $2,000, but have to pay back $2,200. Your effective interest rate with this method is about 10 percent for one year.

However, another approach is the discounted interest method. Instead of adding the charges to the loan amount, they are deducted from the loan amount. If you borrow $2,000, as in our example above, the lender deducts the $200 in advance. You actually receive $1,800 and pay back $2,000. The effective interest rate with this approach is slightly higher, about 11 percent.

The way your interest is calculated is as important as what the rate is.

The Effective Cost of Credit

What is the real cost of borrowing? If you take out a one-year $10,000 loan at 10 percent simple interest (i.e., interest compounded annually), does the $1,000 finance charge really constitute only a 10 percent charge on the use of the money over the full year? Be careful, it is a trick question!

If you pay off the loan in 12 equal monthly payments, you have use of the full $10,000 only for the month before your first payment. If the balance outstanding at the end of the 12-month period is zero, the average balance for the entire period is approximately $5,500. A $1,000 interest charge on the average outstanding balance of $5,500 is actually costing you about 18 percent a year, not 10 percent.

Technical terminology can get very confusing when comparing different ways to figure interest (simple or compounded daily, weekly, quarterly and so on). The Truth-in-Lending Act simplified understanding this mess by requiring lenders to show the A.P.R. (actual percentage rate).

Use the A.P.R. to compare the effective cost of loan proposals to get an accurate idea of the relative attractiveness of the expense entailed repaying the loan.

Before the high inflation and volatile interest rate markets of the 1970s and 1980s, most loans were made at fixed rates. However, as evidenced by the S&L crisis now plaguing the financial markets, many lenders wound up losing heavily. Many lenders, S&Ls in particular, were caught in a credit squeeze due to their practice of making long-term commitments at low interest rates, when their cost of funds varied short-term.

For example, when lenders loaned money on a 30-year mortgage at a 7% interest rate, and their cost of funds was only 4.5%, they made money. When they were locked into a 30-year low-interest loan while their cost of funds skyrocketed to double-digit levels (depositors took money out of passbook savings accounts in search of higher returns), they took huge losses.

The survivors learned from their mistakes. Now long-term loans usually have variable interest rates. This means that the interest rate varies with market rates. When interest rates go up, the interest on your loan rises. When rates go down, the interest you pay on your loan declines.

The way it works is that your loan agreement spells out some formula for the interest charge. Generally, it stipulates that the rate on your loan varies with some index such as the prime rate, the 91-day Treasury bill rate, or various Federal Reserve indices. For example, your loan rate will be set at two points over the bank's prime rate. When the prime rate goes up one point, the charge on your loan will be adjusted accordingly.

Figure 3.1 is a worksheet for calculating the relative cost of adjustable rate and fixed rate loans. Since the procedure is very time consuming to do by hand, step-by-step instructions for doing the calculations on a Hewlett Packard 12C hand-held calculator are included.

Facts:

- ▶ Points for each loan: $3,900
- ▶ Appraisal for each loan: $500
- ▶ Fees for each loan: $1,500

Figure 3.1 (a): Calculating the difference between a five-year adjustable-rate loan and a fixed-rate loan

The following steps are for HP12C financial calculator.
Determine payment on a fixed rate loan of $195,000 for 30 years at 12%.
Step 1	f/CLX	Clears financial calculator
Step 2	Enter 195,000	hit PV
Step 3	Enter 30	hit g/n
Step 4	Enter 12	hit g/i
Step 5	Hit PMT	
	Display $1,985.94	

Your payment is $1,986
Multiply 1,986 x 6 = 11,916
Enter in column Y, first six-month period.

Determine payment on a loan $195,000 for 30 years starting at 8.5%.
Adjust 1% every six months.
Step 1	f/CLX	Clears financial calculator
Step 2	Enter 195,000	hit PV
Step 3	Enter 30	hit g/n
Step 4	Enter 8.5	hit g/i

Display $1,488.80
1,488 x 6 = 8,933
Enter in column (W) first six-month period.
Second 6 months — repeat above steps but change interest trate to:
        9.5% for second six months
        10.5% for third six months
        11.5% for fourth six months
        12.0% for fifth six months

Determine the present value of an amount in the future.
Step 1	f/CLX	Clears financial calculator
Step 2	Enter 8,933	hit PV
Step 3	(Enter number of months from present)	
	Enter 6	hit n
Step 4	(Enter a market rate of 10%)	
	Enter 10	hit g/i
Step 5	Hit PV	
	Display 8,499	

Enter in column (X) 1st 6 month period

Continue this for each number adjusting the months out example.
Step 1	f/CLX	Clears financial calculator
Step 2	Enter 9,761	hit PV
Step 3	Enter 12	hit n
Step 4	Enter 10	hit g/i
Step 5	Hit PV	
	Display 8,836	

Figure 3.1 (b)

	Variable-Rate Loan Payment (W)	Net Present Value of Payment (X)	Fixed-Rate Loan Payment (Y)	Net Present Value of Payment (Z)
Points	3,900	3,900	3,900	3,900
Appraisal	500	500	500	500
Other Fees	1,500	1,500	1,500	1,500
First six Months of Payments	8,933	8,499	11,916	11,337
Second six Months of Payments	9,761	8,836	11,916	10,787
Third six Months of Payments	10,610	9,139	11,916	10,263
Fourth six Months of Payments	11,476	9,404	11,916	9,764
Fifth six Months of Payments	11,916	9,290	11,916	9,289
Sixth six Months of Payments	11,916	8,839	11,916	8,839
Seventh six Months of Payments	11,916	8,409	11,916	8,409
Eighth six Months of Payments	11,916	8,001	11,916	8,001
Ninth six Months of Payments	11,916	7,612	11,916	7,612
*Tenth six Months of Payments	11,916	7,242	11,916	7,242
Total	118,176 (a)	91,171 (b)	125,060 (c)	97,443 (d)

Compare (b) to (d)

The lower number is the cheaper 30-year loan paid off in five years.

* Assumes the variable rate stays the same as the fixed for the next 25 years. Most loans are paid off or refinanced every 5 years.

- Loan terms are 30 years each
- Variable rate loan starts at 8.5% and adjusts 1% every six months and caps at 12%
- Term loan is for 12%
- Net present value used is 10%.

Note: Common sense indicates that the variable rate loan is cheaper because the cap rate is the same as the term rate. However, if the term rate were 11.25 percent, it would be more difficult to determine which loan is cheaper. Figure 3.1 will show you the cheaper loan. Try it yourself!

Other Costs

The interest charge is the most obvious cost. However, you must build other costs into your borrowing decisions. "Points" are up-front charges assessed for most mortgage financing. Using mortgage financing to buy a building for your business, taking out a second mortgage on your business property, refinancing your current mortgage or assuming the mortgage of a business you are buying will all usually cost you points. (One point is equal to 1 percent of the loan amount.)

For example, if you take out a $100,000 mortgage loan and are charged two points, it means you pay $2,000 plus other charges.

Rejecting mortgage loans over other types of financing doesn't mean that you will avoid additional loan fees. When you take out a line of credit loan, even one that is nonbinding, you will usually be charged a "commitment fee" of 1 percent or 2 percent of the credit line. Lenders charge fees in addition to the stated interest charges to cover their costs and profits. "Loan origination," "loan packaging", and "loan processing" fees are some common names for fees.

Banks and other lenders who provide full business services charge different fees for their services. Depending on your relationship with the bank, the fees may vary. If you are in a cash business, banks will charge you for handling coins, bills, checks or other transactions. The fees may be a flat monthly fee or on a "per transaction" basis. It pays to comparison shop not only for the stated interest rates, but for all the other fees that lenders may charge.

Variables in Costs

Several things affect lenders' fees. Commercial banks, especially when extending large loans, often require that borrowers keep "compensating balances" on deposit with the lender. The amount is usually expressed in terms of a percentage of outstanding loan balances. Find out if you get credit for your "free funds" (checking account balances) on deposit with your lender. If you don't ask, don't expect the lender to volunteer any cost-cutting practices. Generally, a depositor will get preferential rates. The longer your relationship with a bank, the better your rates are likely to be.

When a loan agreement is drawn up, banks use legal counsel. Those banks that use in-house counsel will not charge you fees for the legal work (or at least will charge you much less). However, some lenders use outside attorneys to draw up their loan documents. In that case you will usually be charged a fee for legal services.

When evaluating a potential lender, find out what legal fees are charged to borrowers. The fees charged by outside attorneys will be passed along to you, and they can be substantial. Some banks that seem competitive based on interest rates alone may cost more due to other fees and charges they tack onto loans.

> **Points to Remember**
> 1. Finance charges consist of interest and carrying costs.
> 2. Interest charges can be figured as either add-on or discount.
> 3. Most loans are now made with variable interest rate charges that are tied to some index such as the prime rate or the Treasury bill rate.
> 4. Never sign an agreement before you fully understand the fees and charges.

BORROWER BEWARE: LOAN COVENANTS

Lenders usually include restrictions to the loan agreement. These are called loan covenants.

Typical covenants restrict what you can do with your business' money. A fairly common practice is to tie the availability of your line of credit to maintenance of specified financial ratios. The covenant may specify that your company's current or quick ratio be at least 2:1 or 3:1 on a quarterly basis. If the specified ratio falls below, your LOC could be terminated even if you are still making your payments.

Other common covenants limit the amount of salary you can take. This can either be a fixed amount or stated in relation to net income or gross sales, or in some other way.

Frequently it will be stipulated that any money you loan to the business be subordinated to loans from the lender. This means that the lender has first claim on the business's assets in case of default. Your loan agreement may forbid you from borrowing from the business until the loan is paid off.

If your business relies very heavily on only one or two people, a covenant may be added requiring insurance on key employees. A covenant may require that the loan be paid in full before changing banks.

Another common covenant restricts your business from involvement in areas considered high risk. For example, you may be restricted from handling toxic wastes or chemicals.

Covenants are really limited only by the imagination of your lender. Since many of these covenants can impair your flexibility, it is important that you know and understand your loan agreement in its entirety.

SELECTING YOUR LENDER

A long-term stable relationship is beneficial to both parties. When lenders evaluate you and your business for the first time, subjective factors play an important role.

A business that changes banks frequently will not be viewed favorably.

Things to look for when interviewing lenders include:

- ▶ Their experience with your industry.
- ▶ Their lending authority.
- ▶ The right person for your needs.
- ▶ Easy access to a single loan officer who will be in charge of your account.
- ▶ Access to upper management.
- ▶ Sufficient lending limits to serve your needs.

A one-stop banking relationship is usually preferable to spreading out things such as checking, savings, cash and check handling and credit card access.

It is essential that the loan officer understands your business in detail.

PREPARING YOUR BUSINESS PLAN

Your business plan plays a vital role in demonstrating to a lender that you:

- ▶ Have a profitable business
- ▶ Follow good management practices
- ▶ Have growth potential
- ▶ Know what you are doing
- ▶ Keep organized, accurate financial records
- ▶ Manage your cash well
- ▶ Have an asset base
- ▶ Pay your bills in a timely manner.

A written business plan with financial statements prepared by a professional creates the credibility that is so important in the financial world. You can have the greatest business in the world, but if you can't explain what you do, why it is successful and why it will continue to be profitable in the future, you will not be able to get a loan.

Who You Are

It is important to tell a good story about your business. What is it that makes your business such a good business? Tell why your company is unique.

EXAMPLE

You are in the trucking business. Show how your carefully implemented maintenance program results in lower operating costs than for the industry in general or how the types of things you transport afford an advantage for your business.

Show how you have instituted good business practices for administration of the company. How is your marketing organized? Are you using a cash management system that was designed by a professional? What does it mean for your bottom line?

Describe your management team. Lenders like to see experience in management, finance and marketing. If you are a manufacturer, you will need manufacturing experience in your management people. Lack of appropriate (industry-related, or some administrative, finance or marketing) experience is a leading cause for the rejection of small business loan applications. Don't leave anything to interpretation. Enumerate the reasons why your staff, with their respective backgrounds, give you a business advantage.

Detail your company's history. Explain the present position of the company and what you expect for the future. Include plans for more or different products or services or other significant changes you anticipate. You want the loan officer to feel the same kind of confidence and excitement about your business that you do. That is one of the reasons you want to work with a lender who has some experience in your field or at least a related industry. You don't want to be talking to an auto loan specialist about your business needs.

Your Turn

The following should be used to ensure that you cover at least these items in your discussion:

1. What products or services do you provide?
2. What is the pricing structure? How was it determined?
3. What variety do you offer in these products or services (i.e., sizes, styles, quality, support, etc.).
4. Who are your customers? Who uses your product or service? What do they use it for? Why do they buy yours?
5. How is the product or service distributed?
6. What is the marketing plan? (Include public relations and advertising; specify media chosen, independent sales reps, company reps, etc.)

EXAMPLE

You may think that your trucking business is much like others in the area. That won't be very interesting to a lender. Here are just some of the differences that could exist between what on the face appear to be similar trucking companies:

1. *Long-term versus short-term hauling*
2. *Union versus nonunion*
3. *Higher or lower costs due to maintenance program*
4. *Higher or lower operating costs due to employee turnover*
5. *Transporting high-risk toxins or chemicals versus lower-risk car parts or canned food*
6. *Stable, diversified customer base versus overreliance on single customer*
7. *State-of-the-art dispatch and tracking system versus pencils and yellow pads*
8. *Employee training and educational assistance*

Banks do not like businesses that grow too fast. They know from history that rapidly growing companies tend to outgrow their management and sales capability. The idea is to stay within planned growth targets. If your projections show a 25% growth rate and you hit that target, it is okay. However, if you plan a 10% growth rate and then hit 25% or 30%, the lender will get nervous.

What Is the Market?

Your lender wants some idea of your competition. Describe the general marketplace for your product.

What is your market share? For most small businesses, this is simply a comparison of how you do relative to other businesses in the same geographical area. What is the approximate dollar volume, the average rate of growth, and the demand?

Address market trends. Describe the trends in general terms. Relate this information to how your business fits into the picture. Cite published studies by the Chamber of Commerce or government reports to support your statements. You may want to hire an expert to provide statistical support.

Attach relevant documents such as published articles or research reports that relate directly to your business. Remember, unlike a worker who can supply a W2 form to prove steady income, a business's prospects are not so clear cut. You want to establish that the market will indeed be as strong or stronger for you over the life of the loan.

Who Manages the Business?

Poor management or lack of appropriate management experience is one of the chief reasons that lenders reject small business loan applications. Lenders want to know that the management of the business is in good, experienced hands.

Generally, lenders look for some administrative, financial and marketing experience. A primary concern is the typical small business's failure to plan ahead. Advance planning is the key to success, not only in getting a loan but in staying in business.

Emphasize appropriate experience. Show how you or the person in charge of the company's finances understands cash management. Does your financial manager have business or finance degrees or similar experience with another company?

Another factor that is important is work history stability. A key manager who is constantly changing jobs will make your lender worry. Have you made provisions such as "key employee insurance" to cover problems that could arise in the case of disability of key personnel?

Organize the descriptions of your managers' backgrounds to fit lenders' expectations. For example, lenders will want to see experience in three main areas: administration, finance and marketing. In a manufacturing concern, they will want manufacturing management experience.

Often a lender will want to meet your management team personally. The loan officer may want to visit your plant in some circumstances to size up management competence. Speaking directly with your management team will help make the lender feel more involved with the company.

Why Do You Want the Loan?

You need to explain exactly why you need the loan. What you want to show is how the loan fits in with your long-term planning for the business. The loan should be an integral part of your business plans, not an afterthought to bail you out of problems. Be specific. Keep in mind the following legitimate business loan requests, including:

- ▶ Expansion
- ▶ Operating cash to smooth out the difference between your billings and receipt of money
- ▶ Employee training
- ▶ Buying new equipment
- ▶ Financing inventory buildup (e.g., before holiday rush)
- ▶ Buying office or manufacturing space

Financial Statements

The first step in ensuring that the lender views your application positively is providing detailed, organized, comprehensive financial documentation both for yourself personally and for your business.

The lender wants to ensure that your company generates sufficient income to pay for operations, including capital expenditures, interest and principal payments on debt and any dividend payments that are made to stockholders.

The financial statements that you will need to provide for your business include:

- Balance sheet
- Cash flow statement
- Income statement
- Tax returns
- Lender's loan application.

You will always have the dilemma of wishing to show the lowest possible net income on your tax return but the best possible net cash flow for your lender. Experienced lenders recognize the predicament. They understand that a part of intelligent business planning is minimizing your tax burden.

For additional information, the lender may ask you to break down your business's cash flow in a statement of income and expenses or a summary of cash receipts and disbursements. If your company is incorporated, you may be asked for a statement of changes in retained earnings. There are other ways to show a business's income and net worth. Your accountant can prepare any other form that is requested. Submitting financial statements reviewed by your CPA will add credibility with most lenders.

In addition to statements of the current financial condition of your company, you will need to include projections of cash flow for the next five years. Basically, you need to project anticipated income versus expenses to get a net cash flow figure.

Your projections should include the following information:

- The term of the loan
- The specific amount of the needed funds
- Any increased marketing expenses to handle higher sales
- Breakdown of the period during which funds are needed
- Examination of all expenses that may change as a result of the loan.

For the first 24 months you should break these figures down by the month. For the next three years, a quarterly accounting is customary. Naturally, the further into the future you get, the less you or your lender can rely on the figures.

Be sure to show how the loan you are requesting will be repaid. After all, that is the whole reason for this exercise!

Key elements of a good business plan include:

1. Summary of firm
   A. Who you are
   B. How long you've been in business
2. Description of products or services offered
3. Analysis of competition
4. Where you fit in the industry
5. Background information on key personnel
6. Description of operations
7. Report on marketing practices
8. Financial statements

A. Current balance statement and income statement

B. Cash flow projections

9. Exhibits

    A. Marketing materials

    B. Relevant research reports

    C. Expert opinions

    D. Charts

WHAT INTERESTS THE LENDER

Liquidity Ratios

When lenders review your business plan and financial statements, they have a checklist of items to look at. One of the first things they check is a number of financial ratios that your financial statements reveal. These ratios are guidelines for telling lenders whether you will be able to service current expenses plus pay for the additional expense of a new loan.

Lender wants to see how "liquid" your financial position is. They want to see if you generate enough cash from operations to pay for your expenses and still have funds for debt service.

Financial ratios enable the lender to compare your current financial condition with the past and the industry average. Of course, they also tell the lender whether conditions will improve or decline based on your projections of future cash flow.

We will look at three measures of liquidity. These ratios are:

- Current ratio
- A/R turnover
- Inventory ratio

The current ratio measures the short-term solvency of a business. It measures the margin of safety that management builds into its current financial picture.

The formula is:

$$\frac{\text{Current Assets}}{\text{Current Liabilities}}$$

Since current assets consist of liquid assets such as cash and securities, accounts receivable and inventory, lenders look at the specific makeup of the current ratio. For example, a firm that has a greater percentage of current assets in cash than in inventory is considered more liquid. It takes some time for even the most marketable inventory to be liquidated.

In addition, different industries have different standards. Some inventories such as high technology goods are subject to very fast deterioration in value. Other inventories such as tires or auto parts are less subject to severe swings in value.

In addition to measuring a company's cash liquidity, the lender wants to see how proficient your credit and collection policies are. Remember, accounts receivable are an important element in your current assets.

The Accounts Receivable Turnover formula is:

$$\frac{\text{Total Credit Sales}}{\text{Average Net Accounts Receivable}}$$

A common measure of management competence is inventory turnover. This assesses how often your average inventory is sold each year. A high ratio indicates that the inventory is being sold more quickly. That means there is less risk from high storage costs, insurance or the chance that prices will fall while you are still holding the inventory.

The formula is:

$$\frac{\text{Cost of Goods Sold}}{\text{Average Inventory}}$$

Like the other ratios, the inventory turnover ratio varies widely from industry to industry. You should compare your company's performance with the industry you're in. In addition, lenders will look at the history of your company to see if there is improvement or not.

Profitability Ratios

Lenders use other ratios to measure how profitable your business is. Two common profitability ratios are gross profit and net income to sales.

Gross profit is easy enough to understand. It is the difference between sales and the cost of goods sold. The gross profit ratio measures your average profit margin.

The formula is:

$$\frac{\text{Gross Profit}}{\text{Net Sales}}$$

Historical analysis is most valuable with this ratio. It tells you (and the prospective lender) what your company's profitability trend is. A rising trend shows that costs are being kept under control. A declining trend reveals potential problems that management must face.

Net income to sales is an important measure of the company's profitability. The formula is:

$$\frac{\text{Net Income}}{\text{Net Sales}}$$

Debt Ratios

An important consideration for any lender is the question of how much debt you already have. Expect your lender to be interested in how much debt you have relative to net worth. A lower ratio signals a stronger financial position. A lender wants to know that even if income drops somewhat, there is still a cushion.

The debt to net worth formula is:

$$\frac{\text{Total Debt}}{\text{Net Worth}}$$

If your business is incorporated, the common measure is debt to equity:

$$\frac{\text{Total Debt + Preferred Stock}}{\text{Total Stockholder's Equity}}$$

A final ratio is used to evaluate how well your company's income covers its debt obligations. The Times Interest Earned ratio assesses how many times the interest expense of your business is covered by earnings from operations.

The formula is:

$$\frac{\text{Earnings Before Income and Taxes}}{\text{Total Interest}}$$

This ratio tells your lender how well your earnings cover your debt servicing obligations. It also gives bankers a measure of how far your earnings can fall without hurting your ability to repay the loans.

SETTING OFF ALARMS

The higher the ratio, the stronger your position. Lenders generally want to see 3:1 or higher.

When reviewing the documents you submit with your loan application, lenders are primarily interested in seeing that there are no inconsistencies among the documents. They want to ensure that what you report on one document is supported by information you provide on other financial statements.

Tax Returns

The information of particular interest to lenders that your tax returns reveal includes:

- ▶ Interest income
- ▶ Interest expense

- Income history
- Other liabilities such as subsidiary companies or partnerships that may require additional capital infusions.

If you report that your business had an average $30,000 cash balance, that should be confirmed by earning some interest income. It would be very poor cash management if your cash balances are not working for you. If you report little debt, yet your tax return shows a large deduction for interest expense, the lender will be suspicious. You should point out such discrepancies in advance.

If you report a large net income for your business this year compared to earnings in previous years, be prepared to explain why this latest turn of events will continue. Have you developed a new manufacturing method, better marketing, a new product? Lenders will discount a single outstanding year based on the overall track record if there is not a good reason to expect the higher income to continue.

Points to Remember

1. A well-written, concise business plan is vital to obtaining a loan.
2. Your lender must understand what your business is and why it is, and will continue to be, successful.
3. Lenders want to see appropriate experience in your management team.
4. Identify exactly why you need a loan and how much you need.
5. Carefully prepared financial projections that detail how the loan will be repaid are an important element in any business plan.
6. Lenders evaluate business loan requests largely by use of financial ratios to measure liquidity, profitability and ability to service debt.
7. Inconsistencies in your financial documents or simple lack of forewarning about problems will trigger alarms in a lender's review of your loan application.

PRESENTATION

The impression you make on your first serious meeting with a lender is critical. While some of the following items may seem obvious, take the time to go through this checklist before you make your presentation.

Presentation Checklist

- [ ] Be on time.
- [ ] Dress for success. Don't show up in jeans and a T-shirt. Show the lender professional respect.
- [ ] Shake hands firmly.
- [ ] Relax: smile, be friendly.
- [ ] Be courteous. Thank the lender for his/her time and help getting your proposal together.
- [ ] Look at the loan officer. Don't be occupied with notes or paper shuffling. Make him or her the focus of your attention.
- [ ] Listen. Don't dominate conversation. You want to understand exactly what the lender needs to approve the loan.
- [ ] Respond directly to questions. Don't go off on a tangent. Don't be evasive. If you don't know, find the answer in your paperwork, or make a note and get back promptly with the answer.
- [ ] Know how much time your have. Prepare the agenda accordingly. Work through it consistently.
- [ ] Speak positively. Avoid negative comments.
- [ ] Emphasize understanding. Avoid technical jargon. You want the lender to understand the complete picture.
- [ ] Start with the "meat" of your proposal. Don't small talk your way through most of the time you have. Leave minor issues to the end.
- [ ] The best times for meeting are either the first thing in the morning or the last appointment of the day. It is less likely that the loan officer will have to rush to another meeting then.

ASK YOURSELF

- ▶ Do you want a business loan?
- ▶ What types of business loans are available?
- ▶ What do the different types of loans cost?
- ▶ Does the loan cost you more than it is worth?

CHAPTER FOUR

GETTING A PERSONAL LOAN

PERSONAL LOANS

The process of getting a personal loan is very similar to that of getting a business loan. While you do not submit a business plan, you still have the job of demonstrating to the lender that your financial resources are sufficient to repay the loan. Your asset base affords the lender some type of protection.

If you are a W2 employee, the job of proving your current income and probable future income is relatively simple. The lender will check your tax returns for two or three previous years and a current check stub.

If you are a business owner, whether in a partnership or as sole proprietor, your task of proving reliable income will be more challenging.

In this chapter we show you how to overcome potential questions about income and job stability. In addition, we take a look at the most common types of personal loans and the variety of terms offered. You will learn how a lender sizes up your financial condition. We will show you what financial ratios rule their world. Understanding the differences among various lenders and knowing how to minimize your costs will go a long way to making your loan seeking experience a happy one.

THE MOST COMMON TYPES OF PERSONAL LOANS

Personal loans serve a number of purposes. For example, very few people can afford to buy a home without the help of a mortgage loan.

Other loans that are not secured by any asset usually require somewhat higher standards to qualify. These might include consolidation (a single large loan to pay off smaller bills such as credit card balances), medical, education (college or some technical training), furniture, appliances, vacation and so on. Usually the rates on these "signature" loans are higher.

Income tax deductions of interest on loans other than mortgages or line of credit against your home have been phased out. Since 1992, you cannot deduct interest on loans from credit cards or for cars, boats, etc. A home equity loan is your best source of money for these items.

Mortgage Loans

For purposes of illustrating the normal personal loan process, we will focus on getting a mortgage loan. Typically, a mortgage loan is the largest personal loan used by most people. To qualify, you must gather substantive financial documentation. If you have had problems with debt, it is important that you resolve those problems. You will probably need to explain the situation to your lender.

The most a lender is likely to loan on a mortgage is 80% of the appraised value of the house.

If you purchase property mortgage insurance (PMI), your lender may be able to go higher.

When deciding what price home you may be able to qualify for, don't forget to take into consideration the whole panorama of costs over and above the price of the home. For example, a lender will require that you have sufficient homeowner's insurance, be able to pay the real estate taxes, have enough cash to make the down payment, and be able to service your other outstanding debts. All these items can add up to a substantial monthly payment.

A secured loan is one that is backed by a tangible asset. They generally have less stringent qualification requirements than unsecured loans and generally charge lower interest rates than unsecured loans. An unsecured loan has no tangible asset base. It is usually your signature guaranteeing repayment. Also mortgage lenders will typically loan up to 80% of appraised value on an unsecured loan.

HOW A LENDER SIZES YOU UP

Whether you are asked to complete a separate balance sheet and income statement or the lender's application, the lender will cross-check all your financial information. You will usually be asked to submit two or three years' of tax returns. Remember, the lender has access to independent verification of your credit record through a credit bureau report.

Once they have all the financial records in front of them, lenders go through a detailed internal checklist, which produces a numerical score that determines whether you qualify or not. The lender evaluates the documents you submit to confirm that what you have said is true. Their scoring or evaluation checklist is specifically designed to catch any discrepancies.

The Lender's Checklist

Imagine that your lender is examining your last three years' tax returns and your loan application. According to that internal checklist, the lender begins going over the things that need to be cross-checked.

First is your salary. Do the figures reported by you in the loan papers coincide with what you reported on your tax returns? If there is a large discrepancy (you recently were promoted, your bonus was deferred past January 1 for tax reasons, etc.), be sure to explain when you submit your papers.

If your income has increased sharply in the past year, explain the variance from past records before your lender asks. Indicate why the current level is a realistic expectation for the future.

The next step is an examination of other types of income. If you show that you have $40,000 in savings, your interest income as reflected on your tax return should reflect that. If your interest income doesn't confirm your savings balance, you will be asked to explain the difference.

Lenders take extra care to ensure that you have not "primed" your financial condition for purposes of qualifying for the loan. For example, if you borrow $30,000 from your parents merely to make your cash balance look better, a sharp lender will uncover the deception. They want to be sure that you do have sufficient assets to make the down payment without having to borrow elsewhere and winding up with another sizable monthly payment.

If you report sizeable stock or mutual fund holdings, the lender can check your tax return to see what dividends you earn. Another check on a claim of a sizable investment portfolio is the capital gains report. Did you report capital gains? Unless they are a recurring part of your income (i.e., regularly appear over the last two or three years on your tax returns), capital gains as an income source will not be considered very highly.

If you receive or pay alimony, it will show up on your tax return. Your lender will want to see the legal papers. The loan officer will examine the divorce decree for things such as escalation or reduction clauses. What is the term of the settlement? Is there a date the obligation to pay (or the right to receive) ends? The lender will also carefully examine schedule A (itemized deductions), because it can give a lender clues about expenses that wouldn't normally appear on financial statements or through a credit report.

For instance, medical expenses for a family of four typically run about $2,500 annually. If this number is larger, the lender will want details. Is someone in your family seriously ill? Are you having significant health problems? The loan officer doesn't want to be in a situation of granting a loan in anticipation of death or disability by the applicant.

Keep in mind that any claims regarding car payments, car upkeep and other related expenses can be checked through both your tax return and an independent credit report.

If your tax returns reveal that you have claimed moving expenses for the past two years, it signals a question of stability for the lender. Why did you move? Do you anticipate another move soon?

Have your answers ready!

The rise of IRAs in the 1980s left many people with sizable retirement plan assets. However, don't overestimate the value of these plans in the eyes of a lender. If you are 35 years old, your retirement plan assets will be discounted about 50 percent because of the fees and penalties that early withdrawal entails.

If you are nearing retirement age, a lender will value your retirement plan assets much higher. For example, at age 62, if you have accumulated a sizeable retirement plan, a lender will consider it a valuable asset.

If you own more than 20 percent in a business (or businesses), the lender will want more information. Be prepared to show copies of articles of incorporation or partnership agreements. The lender wants to know if you have other potential liability exposure.

When reporting on current debt, give full information. Remember, the lender checks this through your credit report. Show the correct average balance for things such as credit cards or installment loans, the interest rate charge and any other pertinent information. If you show credit card debt of $1,000 yet show interest expense on your tax return of $2,000, the lender will know something doesn't jibe. They know that credit card interest runs about 18 percent to 21 percent, not 200 percent.

If you have an IRS dispute, disclose it immediately. It shows up on your credit report. You can defuse an otherwise disqualifying circumstance by explaining in detail what the problem is and when you expect it to be resolved. If you feel unqualified to interpret your tax return, give your lender your tax professional's name and phone number.

If you own rental property, Schedule E details your income and expenses. You can be sure that this will be closely compared with what you have reported on your other financial documents. A current appraisal of the properties can be helpful.

Retirement and Disability Triggers

If your tax return reveals that you have recently received IRA or pension distributions, a lender will wonder why.

- ▶ Have you recently changed jobs?
- ▶ Was there some emergency that required additional money?
- ▶ What was the emergency and will it impinge on future obligations?

If you have been receiving Social Security benefits, a lender will want to know all the details. Is your spouse or a family member disabled? What medical expenses might be involved? Your lender will want some type of confirmation that the problem is not one that can impair your future financial resources.

Two areas that create concern for most lenders are farm interests and partnership investments. Be prepared to show complete details on the financial impact of both of these investments since they both historically represent potential drains on resources.

Farm Interests

If your tax return lists farm income or expenses, you certainly will be asked for more information. Farms are assets that are often liabilities. The lender will want to know:

- ▶ Do you own land?
- ▶ Is it fully paid for?
- ▶ If not fully paid, what are your financial obligations?
- ▶ Is your farm equipment leveraged?

There is much less concern over farm land that is fully owned. However, if it is leveraged (mortgaged), it could represent potential problems.

Partnership Questions

Partnership investments are a hornet's nest of problems. The lender will want to see your K-1 form. The K-1 is like a mini tax return. Issued by the partnership, it itemizes income (business, interest, etc.) and expenses that pass through to the individual partners. It is attached to your personal tax return when filed with the IRS. The K-1 also includes capital account data; i.e., what your investment is worth according to book value.

For example, if you invest $10,000 in a partnership and it loses a proportionate $2,000 in the first year, your investment would be $8,000—but your percent of ownership will remain the same.

EXAMPLE

If you have partnership interests, it is almost mandatory that you retain a financial professional who can explain the details of the K-1. For example, a businessman, after being rejected for a loan by his bank, said that the sticking point with the lender was the large loss his tax shelter partnership was showing.

It turned out that the tax shelter was a multiple-write-off, highly leveraged real estate deal. He had invested $10,000. The first year the tax shelter spun off $40,000 in losses for him due to depreciation. The lender did not understand that the businessman did not have to come up with $40,000 in cash to cover the loss.

CPAs are able to explain that the losses were paper losses the partnership was designed specifically to generate and that, in fact, the value of the partnerships, due to the appreciation of the building, was actually $12,000, a $2,000 profit over the $10,000 paid.

In addition to the K-1, your lender will also want to see the partnership agreement. The agreement spells out things such as the relative future financial obligations of the partners and also the percentage share of ownership. Is the partner required to pay additional capital calls? Are there any other existing or potential liabilities for the loan seeker?

Verification Guidelines

The lender breaks your income and expenses into three broad categories.

1. What you pay for your house (monthly payments, insurance, real estate taxes)
2. What your debt service obligations are (credit cards, installment loans, auto, boat and other debts)
3. What your taxes and other living expenses total.

It is impossible for us to tell you everything that every lender will ask to see. For example, in some areas of the country, monthly utility bills are a major concern in determining what you can afford on a monthly basis. In the northern part of the country, winter utilities run as much as $400+ a month for some homes. Your lender may require detailed data on those expenses.

> **Your Turn**
>
> *As a general rule, lenders expect shelter (mortgage, insurance and real estate taxes) to be about 25% to 33% of your income. If the shelter expenses exceed that percentage, it will trigger a warning alarm for the lender.*
>
> 1. Are all the financial documents you submitted to the lender verifiable?
> 2. Are you aware that lenders will score your application based on financial information and personal data (number of dependents, employment record, whether you are a homeowner, residence stability, etc.)?
> 3. Have you anticipated potential problem areas and pointed them out with thorough explanations and further documentation?
> 4. Have you reported your true debt status?
> 5. Have you attached appraisals for current value of personal property? Break out personal property to show value of specially marketable items such as coin or stamp collections, jewelry, furs, and so on.
> 6. Have you prepared full documentation for partnerships and farm investments?
> 7. Are you aware that lenders break up financial data to determine your housing obligations, your debt service obligations and your other living expenses.

If you are self-employed, most lenders require a more thorough accounting of your financial condition. You can speed the process with accountant-prepared financial statements. As added support, submit bank statements for yourself and your business, three years' tax records and proof of timely payment over the past 12 months of your current mortgage or rent and business expenses.

When working with sole proprietors, the lender will take your income as reported on your tax returns and add back the depreciation to derive your cash income.

Before making a formal loan application, get a good idea of the lender's qualification requirements (they will vary from lender to lender). Your real estate broker, mortgage broker, loan officer, CPA or tax attorney all work regularly with lenders and should be able to give you a good estimate.

TIPS FOR NON-W2 BORROWERS

If you are close to qualifying, your case could be strengthened somewhat by having your CPA sit down with the loan officer to review some potential overlaps between your personal and business expenses that a W2 worker doesn't have.

Qualifying for a loan as a sole proprietor will be based on what your tax return shows is your income. Think of it as if you were going to sell your business. No intelligent buyer will pay more than what is justified by tax documents. Your business's worth is normally based essentially on what you report to the tax authorities. Income taken "under the table" may not only get you arrested, but will qualify you for a lower loan amount and will cause your business to be sold at a discount.

USING MORTGAGE BANKERS

Finding a lender willing to make you the mortgage loan you need can be a very time consuming and frustrating experience. Your first inclination might be to go to your bank, but if your bank is not an experienced mortgage lender (and not all banks are), you may find that they have little leeway in working with nonstandard borrowers.

If you have recently started your own business, making loan applications can turn into a nightmare of locating obscure documents, responding to frequent questions from more than one loan officer, and so on.

Be prepared ahead of time by keeping all key documents in a single file (see Appendix II). Photocopy all documents you provide to a lender for your files.

A good alternative that will save time and aggravation is to use a mortgage broker. Mortgage brokers sell their knowledge of the market. They know what rates are being offered in any given area. Perhaps even more importantly, they know the details of what each lender wants. Since they work constantly with lenders, they learn the idiosyncracies of each institution. Some lenders may be more flexible in qualifying requirements. Others may require larger down payments, homes of a certain sort, and so on.

The experience and background of mortgage brokers enables them to place your loan with the lender most likely to make the loan. You save all the time and frustration it would take to work with the lenders directly.

The knowledge brokers have of lenders' policies means they may know of unique situations that are not common knowledge to the public.

EXAMPLE

In many areas of the country, banks will not make loans on commercial property for less than $1 million. However, some institutions that do.

Using a reputable mortgage broker can be the best way to go. As with any profession, there are unscrupulous mortgage brokers. First, find out what fees, if any, the mortgage broker charges. Most reputable brokers are paid out of the lender's profits, and you do not have any extra charge. Secondly, size up a mortgage broker as you would a stock broker or real estate broker. Interview them. Steer away from those who promise the moon.

Legitimate mortgage brokers will not pretend to be miracle workers. If your financials do not meet the minimum tests we outline in this chapter, don't expect them to be able to do much. **Beware of mortgage brokers who advertise low rates**, then tell you that the mortgage they can get for you is considerably higher priced.

The best rule of thumb is that if it sounds too good to be true, it is! Be safe rather than sorry. Don't pay any fees in advance. Only work with brokers who are recommended by friends who have used them or by financial professionals.

WHAT YOU CAN BORROW: LOAN GUIDELINES

The first thing to keep in mind in getting a mortgage to buy a house is the difference between list price and appraised value. A lender will loan on appraised value. If you are willing to overpay for a home, be prepared to make up the difference with your down payment. Typically you can expect to get a loan for 80% of appraised value.

If you have found a $200,000 home you wish to buy, most lenders will be willing to loan $160,000. However, they will want to know where your down payment of $40,000 comes from. If the down payment is a gift from a relative, you will need a gift letter signed by the party giving you the money. The lender needs to know that you have no obligation to pay it back.

Below are two financial ratios that you need to keep in mind. The housing ratio is a measure of your income from all sources relative to the monthly housing payment (mortgage plus real estate taxes, insurance and utilities) you need to make. The formula is:

$$\frac{\text{Mortgage + taxes + insurance + utilities}}{\text{Income (from all sources)}}$$

The housing ratio should be between 25% and 33%. In other words, your monthly payments for housing must amount to less than one-third of your monthly income. Generally banks will be stricter (25% to 27%) because they typically keep the loan on their books rather than package and resell it. S&Ls will usually be less restrictive.

As you may have guessed, however, the housing ratio is only a good ballpark number for you to work with. Lenders are also interested in what other debt obligations you have and how you handle them. If you have outstanding debts, you will be obligated to make payments on them. That could affect your ability to repay your mortgage loan.

The debt service ratio is your total monthly income relative to your debt obligations including your monthly housing payment. Simply add up your monthly credit card, installment loan, housing payment and other monthly debt payments. Divide that amount by your monthly income.

The formula is:

$$\frac{\text{Housing Payment + Monthly Debt Payments}}{\text{Monthly Income}}$$

The debt ratio should be no more than 48%. In most cases it should run closer to 38% to 42%. The 48% figure is appropriate only for quite wealthy individuals buying a very expensive home. Lenders realize that if your monthly income is $10,000, and $4,600 is for debt service (46%), you still have $5,400 a month leeway. However, if you earn $2,500 a month, and pay out $1,150 (46%), you are left with a more modest $1,350 to cover all other expenses (food, clothing, medical, education, transportation, taxes, etc.).

Adjustable Rate Mortgage (ARM)

The adjustable-rate mortgage (ARM) provides for changes in the interest rate that is charged on the loan. The interest rate changes are tied to specified interest rate indices. The most common index is the one-year U.S. Treasury security index and the Federal Home Loan Bank District Monthly Cost of Funds. Other common indices are the Federal Home Loan Bank Board (FHLBB) National Average Mortgage Contract Rate for Major Lenders on the Purchase of Previously Occupied Homes; the National Average Cost of Funds to FDIC-Insured Institutions; and the FHLBB Monthly Median Cost of Funds Ratio. Lenders tack on a set amount (e.g., 2%) over the index.

ARMs vary greatly in their terms.

- ▶ Some specify a maximum amount that the interest rate can change per adjustment
- ▶ Others cap the amount your payments can increase; it is important to recognize the difference.

If the interest is capped, you know the maximum level your monthly payments can be if rates rise to the cap.

Your Turn

The following checklist should be consulted when comparing ARMs:

- ☐ How often can the rate change?
- ☐ How much can the rate change?
- ☐ How often can payments change?
- ☐ How much can payments change?
- ☐ What is the term of the mortgage?
- ☐ What index is used?
- ☐ Is there a prepayment penalty?
- ☐ What are the closing costs?
- ☐ What margin is charged over the index?
- ☐ What is the index based on?

It may appear at first glance that fixed-rate mortgages are the only way to go. However, since on the average people sell their homes every 3.5 years, ARMs offered at sharp discounts to fixed rates may be appropriate. These "teaser" rates are offered to attract loans. Typically they will be guaranteed for only 6 months or a year, but if there is a cap that limits the amount the payment can be raised each 12 months the loan may be worthwhile (commonly, caps specify two percent per year with a maximum of six percent over the life of the contract). If you expect to move within four or five years, an ARM may be the way to go.

Other Varieties of Mortgages

Flexible payment mortgages are designed to take advantage of the fact that your income will increase from your early earning years to peak years in your 40s and 50s. It is easier for young home buyers to make smaller payments in the early years of a mortgage. As their incomes rise, they can afford larger payments. Older homeowners are more comfortable with higher payments in their remaining working years and lower payments when they retire.

A biweekly mortgage is a fixed-rate mortgage based on 26 biweekly payments rather than the usual 12 monthly payments. Since you are making more frequent payments, the term of the loan is shortened. This cuts the total interest cost over the term of the loan. For example, a $100,000, 30-year mortgage at 10% paid on a biweekly basis would be paid in full in 21 years. You would save more than $75,000 in interest.

A rate-reduction-option mortgage is a fixed-rate loan that gives the borrower the right to convert to a lower fixed-rate loan within five years. Typically the option can be exercised only if rates have fallen by two percentage points or more.

Fixed or Adjustable Rate

The major loan decision for most home buyers today is whether to pay the higher current rate of a fixed-rate mortgage, or to take an adjustable-rate mortgage (ARM) in the hope that rates will not rise above the fixed rate in the foreseeable future.

In most cases it does not make sense to base your decision on a belief that in 20 years rates may rise like they did in the 1980s. Base your decision on how long you intend to own your home. The average mortgage is paid off every three to five years.

Figure 3.1 in the last chapter is a worksheet to help you decide between fixed- and adjustable-rate mortgages.

Refinancing

In most instances, a home will increase in value over the time that you own it. You can get additional money by refinancing based on the home's increased value. If you decide to go with a fixed-rate mortgage, there is always the chance that rates will drop sharply. Unfortunately, because of the charges that lenders can tack on, it is not possible to say that just because rates have dropped one or two percentage points you automatically should refinance. Your decision should be based on the numbers.

Your Turn

Be diligent in collecting detailed information about all the costs involved. Find out:

- ► How many points are charged for the new loan?
- ► What other transaction costs there will be? These may include closing costs for things you paid for once before such as a loan origination fee, attorney's fees, title search and insurance, recording fees, appraisal, survey, and new credit check.
- ► Can any of these can be eliminated the second time around?
- ► Will any further down payment be required?
- ► Are there prepayment penalties on your current loan?

After you have exact answers to the above questions, the rest is quite straightforward. Subtract the monthly payment of the new loan from your current payment amount. Divide this into the total costs for the new loan. That will tell you how many months it will take to pay these extra costs. Your decision should be based on a realistic estimate of how long you expect to be in the house. It doesn't make sense to refinance if it will take three years to recover your costs and you move in two years.

Some advisors have garnered much favorable press with their recommendations that you can save thousands of dollars in interest charges by taking out 15-year mortgages rather than the usual 30-year note. We advise against that strategy. Take out a 30-year mortgage with no prepayment penalties. If you can pay it off earlier by making additional principal payments each month, then you may want to do so. However, if things get tough—you lose your job, someone in the family has serious medical problems or any of a thousand other unexpected events occur, you will be able to continue making the lower payments. Be sure your loan allows for accelerated principal payments.

Lower payment requirements on the longer-term mortgage may mean the difference between losing your home and credit rating or maintaining both.

1. The housing ratio is a measure of monthly housing expenses divided by income. Most lenders want it to be no higher than 25% to 33%.
2. Your debt service ratio is the total of monthly debt service payments plus housing costs divided by monthly income. Lenders want it to be 38% to 42%. The higher your income, the higher the acceptable percentage.
3. Adjustable-rate mortgages carry variable rate interest charges tied to a specified index. Typical terms include a maximum 2% per year adjustment and 6% maximum over the life of the mortgage.
4. When comparing adjustable and fixed-rate mortgages, keep in mind that the average family sells their home every three to five years.
5. There are ARMs to suit just about any need.
6. When deciding on refinancing, be sure to find out all fees that will be charged. Interest rate differences alone are not enough to tell whether you should refinance.

Until you actually get around to applying for a mortgage loan yourself and see the list of charges in the escrow papers, you may not realize that the interest rate is only one of many potentially quite expensive charges.

Under the federal truth-in-lending laws, points must be figured in the quoted annual percentage rate (A.P.R.). This means that the A.P.R. (**the rate you pay**) is higher than the interest rate specified in the mortgage agreement and usually quoted by lenders.

In this chapter we have dealt mainly with mortgage loans. The process for other personal loans is similar but not usually as complicated. The lender will still request a loan application and verification of income and debt, but may or may not request tax return, etc.

The lender's requirements are still the same in granting a car or boat loan. They have an internal checklist to determine a ratio to see if you qualify.

A good rule of thumb can be taken from the mortgage ratios. Your total debt (including the loan you are applying for) and housing cost should not exceed 48% of your income.

When comparing fixed-rate mortgages, look at the A.P.R.s rather than the more commonly quoted note rate for an accurate comparison. Don't forget about other closing costs.

While points will be the biggest additional loan expense, other fees can add up to a considerable expense. These closing costs may include:

- ▶ Cost of appraisal
- ▶ Loan origination fee
- ▶ Attorney's fees
- ▶ Title search and insurance
- ▶ Recording fees
- ▶ Survey
- ▶ Credit report

ASK YOURSELF

- ▶ Describe the type of personal loan of you want.
- ▶ What does your lender want?
- ▶ Describe the loan qualification process.

CHAPTER FIVE

PREPARING A SELF-AUDIT TO HELP YOUR LENDER

THE IMPORTANCE OF BEING ORGANIZED

Every person and business is unique in some respects. Even though virtually all lenders are motivated by the same desire to make profitable loans to reliable customers, each conducts its business differently. Things that are important to one lender (e.g., type of business, type of loan needed, type of collateral required) may not be for another.

Some lenders make only secured loans to businesses of a certain size within a specific geographical area. Others, in the same area, may make a much wider variety of loans.

You can never be sure exactly what a lender may be seeking when you make your presentation. It is important that you be prepared for just about any type of question. If your business has moved significantly beyond the one-person shop, it is unlikely that you will know every financial detail.

However, if you take the time to organize your paperwork and understand the contents of each item, you will be able to retrieve the requested information quickly. The best way to organize your material is to order it in terms of the forms you are asked by the lender to prepare.

Know the details of your loan proposal intimately. Know:

- ▶ Why do you need the money?
- ▶ What will the money accomplish for you?
- ▶ How does the lender know it will be repaid?

You should put each document and any associated paperwork in a labeled folder. Make sure you can easily read the folder identifier. Get used to replacing the folders in the same order when you consult them (see Appendix II).

SUGGESTED ORGANIZATION PLAN

The specific order of the folders is not as important as consistency in their use. One way to order them:

1. Loan application form and supporting documents
   A. W2 form
   B. Pay check stub

2. Tax returns (two to five years)
   A. All schedules and related tax forms
   B. Divorce decree: alimony and child support details
3. Documents on business interests
   A. Partnership agreement(s)
      1. K-1(s)
      2. Buy/sell agreements
   B. Corporation papers
      1. Articles of incorporation
      2. Buy/sell agreements
      3. Minutes
   C. Farm ownership
      1. History
      2. Detailed records
4. Current cash flow and income statements
   A. Explanatory notes of any unusual items (e.g., term loan ending, alimony termination date, etc.)
5. Balance sheet
   A. Explanatory notes on any unusual items
   B. Appraisals or valuation notes on appropriate assets
6. Business Plan (Key Elements of a Good Business Plan include:)
   A. Summary of firm
      1. Who you are
      2. How long you've been in business
   B. Description of products or services offered
   C. Analysis of competition
   D. Where you fit in the industry
   E. Background information on key personnel

- F. Description of operations
- G. Report on marketing practices
- H. Financial statements
    1) Current B/S and I/S
    2) Cash flow projections
- I. Exhibits
    1) Marketing materials
    2) Relevant research reports
    3) Expert opinions
    4) Charts

THE IMPORTANCE OF SELF-AUDITING: KNOW YOUR WEAKNESSES

Familiarize yourself with every important detail of your business and potential problem areas that you need to address. Naturally when preparing your documentation and making your presentation, you want to emphasize your strengths. Your main thrust is to show why you will be able to repay the loan. Lenders have devised their research methods to ferret out problems. The best way to handle this is to be prepared ahead of time by identifying what areas may raise questions regarding your financial condition (current or future) or your debt paying track record.

Your Turn

Review your documents with these three tests in mind.

1. Are there any cash flow items that may raise questions?
2. Are there any problems in your credit history?
3. Are your assets encumbered in any way?

The relative success of lenders depends to a great degree on their ability to distinguish good risks from bad. They have more experience spotting potential problem areas than you do covering them up.

Examples of cash flow problems

1. Fluctuating income
2. Inconsistencies between interest income and identifiable interest-earning assets
3. Short earning history
4. Discrepancy between W2 or tax return income and claimed income
5. High interest expense
6. Large potential debt exposure (e.g., credit lines)
7. Cosigner or guarantor on loan
8. Escalating alimony or child support agreement

Examples of credit history problems

1. Occasional late payments
2. Chronic late payments
3. Failure to pay
4. Credit disputes (e.g., refusal to pay for allegedly defective product that was purchased on credit, dispute over amount charged, etc.)
5. Judgments
6. Bankruptcy

Examples of problems with your assets

1. Undisclosed liens on listed assets
2. Asset not really owned by you (e.g., temporary cash loan from relative to make your financial statement look better)
3. Assets actually co-owned
4. Assets overvalued
5. Problem assets: negative cash flow rental property, farms, etc.
6. Legal commitments for additional cash infusions (e.g., partnership agreements or investment contracts)

As you do your self-audit, note all the items that may present a problem. If you are in doubt, include it on your list. Once completed, make notes for your own reference on each item. You will now be in a position to explain any problems.

Income

If your income in the last year is significantly more than in previous years, explain why the current figure is the correct one for figuring your ability to pay in the future.

Another area that may need explaining is a discrepancy between interest income claimed and that shown on your tax return. For example, if you own tax-exempt municipal bonds, the interest income won't show up on your federal tax return. Explain that.

If you paid off a significant amount of debt last year, your tax return will show high interest expense, even though your application does not reflect the same numbers.

You will be asked to provide documentation on:

- Divorce settlements
- Partnership agreements
- Loan for which you are the cosigner or guarantor. You will be asked for information about the other party. Include explanatory notes about the loan, its purpose and who is responsible for the payments.

If you are a cosigner or guarantor for a loan, financial information on the other party should be included if they are making the payments.

Credit Record and Asset Problems

Personal property such as art or other collectibles are automatically devalued by as much as 50%. One way to head this off is to include appraisals. If you do not have a current appraisal, attach an explanation of how you arrived at the values, including sales price plus cost (e.g., spoke to XYZ Art Gallery, advised by Sotheby's auction house, etc.).

If you are buying a house and need $40,000 for the down payment, your lender will be reviewing your financial documents with an eye to understanding where you will get the money. If your down payment is a gift from a relative, you should attach a gift letter confirming that **you have no obligation to repay the money.**

The credit report on you that the lender requests will show any liens that are public record. The value of your assets is reduced by the amount of outstanding liens.

Many people are surprised to see that a dispute they thought had been resolved shows up on their credit report. For example, if you refuse to pay a bill due to defective product or service by a vendor, it may show up as a failure to pay on your credit record. You can attach an explanation to your credit report.

Points to Remember

1. Keep a complete photocopy of all documents given to the lender.
2. A thorough self-audit should be completed before turning any paperwork over to a lender.
3. A self-audit will familiarize you with the important financial details and reveal potential problem areas.
4. Point out and explain problems before the lender uncovers them.
5. There are four major areas of concern for your lender: ability to pay, credit history, quality of assets and secondary source of repayment.
6. Include explanatory notes for any items that may pose problems.
7. If there is anything unusual about your income (fluctuates widely, jumped significantly recently, etc.), include some explanation.
8. Don't ignore credit history problems. Explain late payments (you were on vacation or ill, etc.) before they turn up for the lender on your credit report.

BUILD ON YOUR STRENGTHS

While it is important that you address problem areas with your lender, we certainly don't mean for you to dwell on them. You want to orient your proposal and presentation to your strengths. Those strengths may be in one or more areas.

For business loans, an area that carries weight with lenders is management experience. Even if you have not owned your business for several years, as long as you have been in the same type of business or industry for some years, that is a valuable asset.

The composition of your management team can score points.

Lenders want to see that your management team is skilled in the areas that any business needs. Lenders want to see that in addition to having sales or marketing ability, someone in your business who understands how to cope with production details. If you are manufacturing a product, who is in charge of operations? What is their educational background and work experience?

Naturally, lenders are interested in who is in charge of the financial details. Highlight the financial or cash management experience of yourself or the appropriate members (treasurer, CFO) of your management team.

Of course, you shouldn't neglect marketing expertise. Experienced marketing executives who understand the need for controlling costs in the pursuit of sales are an invaluable part of any management team.

Show your lender that your management team has expertise in both financial operations and marketing functions. If you are a manufacturer, underscore your production management experience also. Attach résumés for each member of the team.

Another area of strength is a unique product or service. Feature this advantage prominently. Why is it unique? Explain why there is and will continue to be good demand. Focus on why you are in the best position to take advantage of the market.

If you have a particular edge because of costs (e.g., state-of-the-art production equipment), accentuate it. Can you show that as your business has grown you have controlled costs? Does your company have good name recognition in your market area? That could be a strong selling point. Is your company positioned to take advantage of coming trends (e.g., environmentally sensitive product or service)? Will political developments benefit your company (e.g., zoning, government regulations that require a service you offer, etc.)?

Your strongest suit is your financial condition. Do you have substantial marketable assets (e.g., trucks, cars, tractors, construction equipment, etc,)? Lenders who see that their money is well secured are more comfortable in approving loans.

MAKING AN EFFECTIVE PRESENTATION

We cannot overemphasize how important your first impression on the lender is. Too often people think that there is some magic formula known only to a select few for getting a loan. It is much more mundane than that. All it takes is thorough preparation, good organization and a confident, responsive presentation.

Briefly, these are the major elements of a good presentation:

1. Be prompt. It is better to be early.

2. Dress appropriately.

3. Be friendly. Smile. Demonstrate a firm handshake.

4. Be aware of your body language. Look at the loan officer. Be alert.

5. Have your presentation outlined. Begin with the most important points: what you need, why you need it and how it will be repaid.

6. Listen! Find out exactly what the lender wants. Your loan officer's questions and comments will tell you what is most important. You may be surprised.

7. Respond directly to enquiries. Don't be evasive. If you do not know the answer, write down exactly what you need. Tell the lender when you will get the answer. Follow up as you said.

8. Show respect and trust. Create and build on rapport.

9. When speaking, make sure the lender understands what you are saying. Don't get confusingly technical. Avoid specialized jargon.

10. Find out when you can expect a response.

PRACTICE MAKES PERFECT

A common mistake you can make, particularly if you hire someone to prepare your documents, is to understand poorly what each document contains and its relevance to your loan proposal.

Since a vital component of the whole process is your personal presentation, take the time to practice. The following questions will help you prepare your presentation so that you are comfortable and confident. That first impression can mean a lot.

1. Do you present yourself as a competent, relaxed professional?

2. Do you have the information that is expected?

3. Are you familiar with the operational and financial details of the business?

4. Do you listen and respond to the questions asked?

5. Do you respond directly and succinctly to specific enquiries?

Imagine the contrast between a loan applicant who can confidently answer yes to each of these checkpoints and one who shows up bedraggled, anxious, fumbling for answers and disorganized.

ASK YOURSELF

- ▶ Do you consider yourself organized?
- ▶ List what you believe to be your weaknesses.
- ▶ How will you increase the effectiveness of your presentation?

CHAPTER SIX

IF YOU GET TURNED DOWN

WHAT TO DO

Despite careful planning, close adherence to each step we have outlined for preparing your loan application and a good oral presentation, you may get turned down anyway. It can happen to anybody.

Any number of things may go wrong. Major lenders often get credit reports from more than one bureau. Perhaps erroneous information that you did not know about was in a credit report. New government regulations might affect the approval. Before you try again, it is vital that you find out why you were denied in the first place.

When talking with your lender after being turned down for a loan, project calm professionalism. Agitated badgering of the loan officer can do no good and possibly much irreparable harm.

Written Response

Request that the lender detail in writing the reasons for the denial of the loan. The letter should specify which credit reports were used in evaluating your application. It should also tell you the primary reason(s) for the denial.

You are entitled to a free copy of any credit report that was used by an institution that denied you credit. The institution is required to provide the name and address of credit bureaus it used in evaluating your loan.

Questions to Ask

Talk with the loan officer you have been working with. Ask:

- ▶ Was the loan amount inappropriate? Does the loan request exceed legal lending limit?
- ▶ Was the problem in your presentation? Did you not know answers to questions about costs and profits?
- ▶ Are there any questions or problems about your business's financial status and projections?

- ▶ Are you talking to the right loan officer?

The primary cause for being turned down is a lack of understanding of the business and its prospects. Talk with the loan officer to see if this is the problem. Find out:

- ▶ Is the lender comfortable with your business?
- ▶ Does the lender recognize what is unique about your business?
- ▶ Does the lender prefer manufacturing or service-oriented businesses?
- ▶ Is experience a problem? Would your lender be more likely to approve a loan after six or nine more months of good business?
- ▶ Do they understand your management team's expertise? Is there something missing in terms of managerial experience?

Go to a Higher Level

If you are convinced, after careful review of all information, that the loan was denied improperly, ask to speak to someone at the lending institution with greater authority. Be very careful here, though. You don't want to create hard feelings with your original loan officers, because they may seek to discredit you with the greater authority.

Finally, ask whether another lender might be appropriate. Another lender may be more familiar with your industry.

ARE YOU USING THE RIGHT INSTITUTION?

Not all lenders are the same. Each has its own unique characteristics. We have summarized some of the key differences among lenders.

Retail Banks

Retail banks are oriented primarily to consumer business. Distinguishing features include:

- ▶ Multiple locations (branches)
- ▶ Emphasis on banking services for individuals (e.g., checking and savings accounts, C.D.'s, credit cards, safe deposit boxes, etc.)
- ▶ Oriented to the community (e.g., offering higher C.D. rates in a retirement community; emphasizing overall financial service relationship in a younger neighborhood)
- ▶ Typically lower lending limits (e.g., $100,000 okay but $500,000 would be beyond the scope of most branches)
- ▶ Loan officers "personal service" oriented
- ▶ Portfolio (keep on books) mortgage loans: usually higher cost
- ▶ Typical loans: car, boat, small equity
- ▶ Larger retail operations concentrate commercial operations in regional offices (e.g., Bank of America, Chase Manhattan, Citicorp).

Commercial Banks

Commercial banks are oriented to providing services to businesses. Distinguishing features include:

- ▶ Handling larger loans (e.g., $1 million regularly handled.)
- ▶ Fewer locations (e.g., regional banking center or main branch rather than numerous branches handling transactions)
- ▶ Lender has greater understanding of business and financial matters
- ▶ Emphasis on long-term business relationships; a more direct relationship between loans and deposits.

Savings and Loan Associations

S&Ls have experienced the most changes in recent years of all conventional lending institutions. Specifically created to meet the need for mortgage loans, the deregulation of the financial markets and the resultant volatility in interest rates have caused problems for many S&Ls. Many S&Ls have branched out to nonmortgage lending, but home loans are still their core business. Distinguishing features include:

- Taking deposits from consumers
- Primarily making consumer real estate loans
- Not as experienced with consumer or commercial loans (e.g., cars, lines of credit, other term loans)
- Not business oriented
- Packaging and resale of mortgage loans: usually slightly lower rates than banks.

Finance Companies

Finance companies raise money from investors, banks and other money market sources rather than by taking deposits. Three different varieties exist.

1. Consumer or small loan companies lend money to consumers under the "small loan" laws of each state.
2. Sales finance or acceptance companies buy retail and wholesale debts from automobile and other capital goods dealers.
3. Commercial finance or commercial credit companies make loans to manufacturers secured by inventory, A/Rs or equipment.

Distinguishing features include:

- Consumer finance companies make loans on things they are willing to buy (specific collateral)

- ▶ If borrower defaults, they repossess and resell the collateral, making the fees paid up front as profit
- ▶ Typically, they carry substantially higher fees and/or interest rates
- ▶ They have lower qualifying requirements than banks.

Credit Unions

Credit unions are nonprofit cooperative savings organizations. The members own the institution. Members have a common bond (same employer, same neighborhood, same union, etc.). Distinguishing features include:

- ▶ An informal, close-knit environment (there are some very large credit unions but the norm is smaller organizations)
- ▶ Consumer services such as savings, checking, time deposits
- ▶ Smaller and consumer oriented loans; a $5,000 limit on signature loans is not unusual
- ▶ Lower loan rates than banks because of tax ad-vantages.

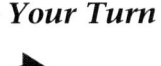

Your Turn — *Review the different types of lending institutions. Which one suits your needs and why?*

If you have been turned down for a loan, you might consider trying a different institution. S&Ls, finance companies and credit unions are usually less stringent in their qualifications than banks.

Whether or not you choose a different lending institution, before you begin reapplying, examine the whole transaction you have just been through. Was the personality mix right? Did you feel that you had established a rapport with the proper lending officer?

Most importantly, did the lender understand your business? Is there anything you could have done to make more clear the unique advantages your business has (state-of-the-art cost control procedures, advanced cash management procedures, landing a large contract, etc.).

HOW TO STRENGTHEN YOUR HAND

Analyze your business with an eye to tightening up collections and minimizing costs to generate increased cash flow.

Is there any way to boost your cash flow? Are you implementing good cash management procedures? Consider these six items.

1. Billing procedures. Do you bill promptly?
2. Can you generate cash more quickly by offering discounts for payment on delivery?
3. Are you investing excess cash quickly to earn interest?
4. Are you carrying customers who are perpetually late payers?
5. Are you experiencing production or shipment delays?
6. Are your collection procedures adequate?

These are only a few of the things that should be taken into consideration. The idea is to review your operations with an eye to fixing loopholes that are costing you money. Try to match your cash inflows with outflows.

Using Outside Help

A letter of credit is an instrument from another person or business, which basically acts like a cosigner or guarantor.

Offer to post a letter of credit.

You would need to "rent" the letter of credit from another person or a business. They would obtain it from a bank, which will charge them about 1% of the amount of the letter of credit. Figure it will cost you another 3% to 5% of the letter of credit amount to the person or company you are renting it from.

It is up to you to calculate whether the expense of using the letter of credit makes economic sense to you. A $100,000 LOC that costs $5,000 over one year may or not make good sense.

HOW FINANCIAL PROFESSIONALS CAN HELP

If you have not used a CPA as an integral part of the loan process, you may want to consider retaining one. The lender is more inclined to accept financial figures that have been prepared by a CPA. This credibility in the eyes of the lender may make the difference between getting a loan and being denied. A CPA can explain in detail any questions about your tax returns.

Since you generally want to show the highest income for a lender but the lowest for tax purposes, having someone there to explain the difference can prove valuable.

In many circumstances, a CPA can explain the full impact of various regulatory or tax rulings to a lender not conversant with the technical details. For example, if you invested in a tax shelter partnership that generated substantial tax losses, those numbers would be reflected on your tax return, even if you didn't actually have to pay cash out of your pocket.

When explaining the details of how cash flow projections were determined, the added credibility of a third-party professional can make the difference between the lender accepting the figures or doubting them.

Just as a writers should not proofread their own work for errors, business owners can miss important details when they review their own operations. A third-party professional may be able to pick up on problem areas.

Your cash flow numbers may be hurt by things such as:

- ▶ Slow A/R payments
- ▶ Poor asset management
- ▶ Poor cash management
- ▶ Too much insurance of the wrong type
- ▶ Under-used assets
- ▶ Inadequate cost controls.

When you write your business plan, it is important that all elements are tied together: business, business prospects, financials, cash flow, and loan repayment allowances. A CPA can help tighten up your business plan in order to direct attention to the important details without overwhelming the lender with mounds of paper. No lender wants to plow through pages of material just to find a few kernels of useful information.

It may be appropriate that you get independent professional appraisals. Include these with your application in the appropriate places.

Appraisals of equipment that will serve as collateral are important. It will also help to have expert opinions on other items such as business trends and prospects, real estate valuations, etc.

Your Turn

When you practice your presentation, use your CPA, who will know what types of questions lenders are liable to ask. CPA's know what information is important on your application. Have them play devil's advocate with tough questions.

1. Can a CPA can help add credibility with lenders?
2. Has your CPA reviewed business operations and made recommendations on managing cash and credit?
3. Have you practiced your loan application with your CPA?
4. Are you using the CPA to explain unusual items on your financial statements?

ASK YOURSELF

- ▶ If you were turned down for a loan, explain why.
- ▶ What are the key characteristics of the following: Retail Banks, Commercial Banks, Savings and Loans, Finance Companies and Credit Unions.

CHAPTER SEVEN

SBA LOANS

SMALL BUSINESS ADMINISTRATION

The Small Business Administration (SBA) is a federal agency formed in 1953 to act as an advocate and to provide financial assistance and advice for small businesses. Historically, the SBA has been seen as a lender of last resort to small businesses that could not otherwise qualify for loans from conventional lenders. That image is not accurate. For the vast majority of SBA loans, the qualifying standards are much like those for conventional loans.

Another major misconception is that SBA benefits are confined to special interest groups such as the handicapped, economically disadvantaged minorities or veterans. While some programs are specifically designed for these groups, the funding for these is considerably less than for its nonrestrictive small business activities.

A major problem encountered by many small businesspeople when working with the SBA in years past was the red tape and consequent long delays in getting approval. The SBA has instituted a number of programs in recent years in an attempt to address those complaints, including the **certified lender** and **preferred lender** programs.

A major advantage of the SBA program is that approximately 30% of SBA loans are targeted for start-up operations. This is a major source of debt financing for new businesses, since banks and other conventional sources of loans typically do not make loans to fledgling companies.

THE VARIETY OF SBA LOANS

The two primary types of SBA loans are guaranteed loans and direct loans. **Guaranteed loans** constitute the vast majority of SBA loans. With a guaranteed loan, a bank or other approved lending source funds the loan with the SBA providing a federal government guarantee of 70 percent to 90 percent of the debt amount. You submit the loan application directly to the lending institution. The lender makes an initial review. If acceptable to the lender, it forwards the application to the SBA. Once the SBA approves it, the lender processes the loan and disburses the funds.

The maximum amount for the guaranteed portion is $750,000. The average size of a guaranteed loan is $175,000 with an average maturity of eight years. Maturity for some real estate loans can be up to 25 years.

SBA funding for direct loans is limited. Usually these funds are available only for specially targeted borrowers such as disabled vets, the handicapped or economically disadvantaged minorities.

Special Loan Programs

In addition to the standard guaranteed and direct loans, the SBA special loan programs.

1. **Small General Contractor Loans** assist small construction firms with short-term financing. Loans proceeds can be used to finance residential or commercial construction or rehabilitation of property for sale. Proceeds from SBA loans cannot be used for owning and operating real estate for investment purposes.

2. **Seasonal Line of Credit Guarantees** provide short-term financing for small firms with seasonal loan requirements.

3. **Energy Loans** fund firms engaged in manufacturing, selling, installing, servicing or developing specific energy measures.

4. **Handicapped Assistance Loans** are for physically handicapped small business owners and private nonprofit organizations that employ handicapped persons and operate in their interest.

5. **The Export Revolving Line of Credit** guarantees to provide short-term financing for exporting firms that have been in existence for one or more years for the purpose of developing or penetrating foreign markets.

6. **The International Trade Loan** guarantees up to $1 million for the acquisition, construction, renovation, modernization, improvement or expansion of productive facilities or equipment to be used in the United States in the production of goods and services involved in international trade.

7. **Disaster Assistance Loans** assist businesses and homeowners in the case of natural disasters such as hurricanes, tornados or earthquakes. Two types of loans can be made:

   A. **Physical disaster loans** to homeowners, renters, businesses and nonprofit organizations located within the disaster area to repair or replace damaged or destroyed homes, personal property and businesses

   B. **Economic injury disaster loans** to small businesses that suffer substantial economic injury because of the disaster. Proceeds may be used for working capital and for paying financial obligations, which otherwise could not have been made due to the disaster.

8. **Pollution Control Financing** assists those small businesses needing long-term financing for planning, design and installation of pollution control facilities or equipment.

7A SBA Loans

The 7A SBA program is the most common form of SBA loan. A 7A loan can be used for most general purposes, including:

- Working capital
- Machinery and equipment
- Furniture and fixtures
- Leasehold improvements
- Land, building and acquisition or construction

Typical maturities for 7A loans are:

- Working capital: seven years
- Machinery and equipment, furniture and fixtures, and leasehold improvements: 10 years
- Land and building: up to 25 years

SBA 502/504 Loans

The SBA's Office of Economic Development offers the 502/504 loan program. Eligibility for these loans is tied to the amount of expanded employment that will result from the investment. In the 504 program, eligible companies may borrow up to a maximum of second deed for 40% of project. The purpose of the 502 program is to buy fixed assets such as land, buildings, machinery, equipment and certain leasehold improvements. It can also be used to finance new construction. The loan carries a maximum guarantee of 85% to 90% of the loan to the participating lender, up to a maximum amount of $750,000 for any one borrower. The percentage depends upon the loan amount (e.g., 90% for less than $155,000).

The 504 program is designed for businesses with a net worth of less than $6 million and annual after-tax profits of less than $2 million. Real estate companies, developer/landlords, the media, financial institutions and not-for-profit corporations generally do not qualify.

In the case of 504 loans, banks finance 50%; the SBA funds up to 40% (up to $750,000) by issuing 100% guaranteed debentures (bonds) sold in the capital market and the borrower must come up with 10%. Usually the borrower secures the financing by working through a certified development company (CDC).

The requirements for these programs are considerably more complex than those for 7A loans. There are requirements of increasing employment, for example. An SBA-CDC acts as an independent loan packager to assist and service interested parties in acquiring government guaranteed loans. If you feel that a 502/504 loan may be appropriate for your business, contact a local CDC. The SBA will provide lists of CDCs by geographical region.

Points to Remember

1. Guaranteed loans are funded by a lender and guaranteed by the SBA.
2. Guaranteed loans constitute most of SBA loans.

3. Direct loans are funded by the SBA only after you have been turned down by other loan sources.
4. Direct loan funding is very limited relative to guaranteed loans.
5. Guaranteed loans are available up to $1 million.
6. Direct loans are limited to $150,000.
7. Special SBA loan programs are available to meet unique needs such as small contractor or seasonal cash flow fluctuations.
8. 7A SBA loans are for most general purposes including:
   A. Working capital
   B. Equipment
   C. Land and building
9. 502/504 SBA loans are tied to the economic benefits they provide the community.

COSTS OF SBA LOANS

SBA guaranteed loans are generally at variable interest rates. Typically, interest rates vary between the prime rate plus 1.5% to 2.75%. The SBA does not allow lenders to assess points at the close of escrow.

However, the SBA does assess a **guarantee fee** of 2% of the amount of the loan that is guaranteed. In other words, if you are approved for a $100,000 loan of which 90% is guaranteed, the loan guarantee fee will be $1,800.

Lenders may also charge a **processing fee** that runs from $300 to $1,500. Remember, the lender must complete all the SBA paperwork and then follow through in each step of the process to ensure timely approval. If you have all the paperwork completed by a qualified third party (e.g., CDC), the processing fee is called a **loan packaging fee**.

When researching SBA loan packaging firms (CDCs), ask if prequalification is available. A legitimate loan packager or lender should offer a prequalification service to establish your potential SBA eligibility before assessing their full fee. This prequalification service should give you feedback on the strengths and weaknesses of your proposal before you spend too much money on the effort.

Usually variable rate loans have no prepayment penalties. They may be prepaid in part or in full at any time without penalty, if proper notice is given to the lender. If you partially prepay the loan, it is automatically reamortized over the remaining term. However, be sure to check with the lender. Fixed-rate loans usually have some type of prepayment penalty. For example, on the SBA 504 loan program, you are charged a prepayment penalty if the loan is prepaid within the first 10 years.

The SBA and most lenders require collateral. If available, this may be in the form of a mortgage on personal or business real estate, security interest in equipment, inventory and/or accounts receivables. The SBA also requires personal guaranties from all principal owners. This is to ensure that the owners have a substantial stake in the company's success.

How SBA Terms Compare

The most important feature of SBA loans is that they typically offer **better terms** than conventional loan sources. Smaller down payments, longer maturities and competitive rates mean lower payments.

SBA 7A loans require a lower down payment (typically 10% for real estate). Generally you can get longer terms. For example, a working capital loan can usually be made for seven years rather than the three years that a conventional lender may provide.

Better terms translate into higher leverage since you can keep your debt service payments lower by spreading them out over time.

EXAMPLE

Real estate financing represents a good example of this leverage. A typical 7A SBA loan may require only 10% down payment with a 25 year term at rates often as low as 1.5% over prime.

Points to Remember

- Most SBA loans charge variable interest rates ranging from prime plus 1.5% to plus 2.75% maximum. There is no ceiling for loans processed under the preferred lender program (PLP).
- The SBA assesses a guarantee fee of 1% to 2% of the amount of the loan guarantee.
- Lenders or loan packagers will charge from $300 to $1,700 for putting together all the paperwork.
- The SBA requires collateral, if available, for its loans.
- SBA terms, such as maturity, are more liberal than those available with conventional loans.
- SBA real estate loans are offered with as little as 10% down payment requirements.

Your SBA application will include the same material as the conventional loan application with the additional SBA paperwork completed. Be sure to include:

- Business plan that includes the amount and purpose of the loan
- Current business balance sheet
- Income statements for the current year and the three most recent fiscal years
- Personal financial statements for owners and any partner or shareholder owning 20% or more of the business
- Statement of collateral including estimated market values
- Résumés of company management

> New businesses should also include:
> - ► An estimated balance sheet specifying the amount of personal investment
> - ► A projection of earnings and expenses for at least one year, showing monthly cash flows
>
> Your lender may require you to submit semiannual and annual financial statements for the life of your SBA loan.

TWO PRIMARY CONSIDERATIONS

The two primary considerations in getting an SBA loan are eligibility and loan sources. Below we have detailed the most important factors for each.

Eligibility

The SBA's broad definition of small business—"... one which is independently owned and operated and is not dominant in its field"—encompasses about 95% of all businesses. However, to be eligible for SBA loans and other assistance, businesses must meet specific size standards. For example:

- ► Wholesale businesses are limited to 100 employees
- ► Service firms can have an annual income ranging from $3.5 to $14.5 million, depending on the industry
- ► Retailers can have an annual income of $3.5 to $23.5 million, depending on the industry
- ► Construction firms' annual income may not exceed $9.5 to $17 million, depending on the industry
- ► Special trade construction firms are limited to $7 million.
- ► Agricultural firms may not exceed $500,000 to $3.5 million in annual income, depending on the industry
- ► Manufacturer's eligibility is limited, depending on the number of employees and type of product produced

Since you will not usually meet with SBA officials, your written business plan must be brief and effective in selling your company.

In addition to meeting these size requirements, a loan applicant must be considered an acceptable credit risk. The SBA stipulates that applicants must:

- Be of good character
- Demonstrate management expertise and commitment
- Have sufficient capital to operate on a sound financial basis
- Have a significant personal investment in the firm
- Demonstrate that future earnings will be sufficient to repay the loan
- Provide personal financial statements, a personal history, company financial statements and a summary of collateral

Ineligible Companies

Some types of companies are not eligible for SBA funding. This includes companies that affect public opinion such as publishing or educational establishments, not-for-profit organizations, theaters and firms engaged in speculation or investment in rental real estate.

SBA LENDERS

Virtually any licensed lender can make SBA loans. However, if the lender is not experienced in SBA procedures, you are likely to experience long delays. Remember, after you file a loan application with a bank, it reviews the proposal. It is then forwarded to the SBA. The SBA can take three days to three or more months to process the application. If something is missing, it can mean a further delay. It can be months from the time your lender contacts the SBA for the first time until funds are dispersed.

The SBA has initiated two programs to reduce this potential time lag—certified lenders and preferred lenders (see Appendix IV).

A **certified lender** is a bank or licensed nonbank lender that is experienced in processing SBA guaranteed loans; it handles most of the paperwork that is required. In exchange for handling most of the needed paperwork hassles, the SBA promises a certified lender that it will **review the loan application and render a decision within three days.**

A **preferred lender** is a bank or licensed nonbank lender that has had extensive experience processing and handling SBA loan applications. It has been a certified lender for at least 12 months. It authorizes fund approval without prior SBA approval. The SBA reviews the loan applications after the fact. A preferred lender handles all loan servicing.

There are approximately 600 certified lenders and 100 preferred lenders nationwide. SBA loan credit qualification requirements are essentially the same as for conventional loans. SBA eligibility requirements vary from industry to industry.

Publishing and educational establishments, not-for-profit organizations and real estate investment are not eligible for SBA loans. A reinvestment firm could qualify, but investments in real estate do not qualify.

A certified lender should get an answer from the SBA within three weeks of filing an application. A preferred lender can approve and fund an SBA loan in-house.

TYPICAL SBA REQUIREMENTS

Start-ups generally have better success in acquiring SBA loans as long as their financial projections look stable and owners are able and willing to use their home or other real estate as collateral.

Typical requirements for a start-up include:

- ▶ A good business story (the same as in dealing with conventional lenders)
- ▶ A one-third capital infusion by the principals
- ▶ Appropriate experience in the industry
- ▶ Well-rounded management experience: operations, finance and marketing

Another common use of SBA financing is to buy an existing business. You will need to meet these requirements:

- ▶ Your capital infusion must be at least one-third of the transaction price
- ▶ There must be collateral either in the form of real estate or in the company's assets, inventory or receivables.

SMALL BUSINESS INVESTMENT COMPANIES

The SBA licenses, regulates and provides financial assistance to privately owned and operated Small Business Investment Companies (SBICs). Their major function is to make the venture or risk investments that are often so difficult for small businesses to obtain. They supply equity capital and extend unsecured loans and loans not fully collateralized to small enterprises that meet their investment criteria.

SBICs are privately capitalized and obtain financial leverage through the SBA. They are profit-making corporations. Due to their own economics, SBICs do not make very small investments.

SBICs finance small firms in two general ways: straight loans and/or equity participation investments.

Equity participation investments give the SBIC actual or potential, full or partial ownership of a small business.

Many SBICs provide management assistance to the companies they finance.

The SBA also licenses specialized types of SBICs to help small businesses owned and managed by socially or economically disadvantaged persons. This type of SBIC is a Section 301(d) SBIC, formerly referred to as a Minority Enterprise SBIC (MESBIC).

WHERE TO GET MORE INFORMATION

The address for the central office of the SBA is Mail Code 2550, 1441 L. Street, NW; Washington, D.C. 20416. It does not handle loan applications directly but can provide appropriate contact information.

The SBA has ten regional offices in major cities around the country: Boston, New York, Philadelphia, Atlanta, Chicago, Dallas, Kansas City, Denver, San Francisco and Seattle. These offices do not make individual loans or offer specific assistance to individuals or businesses. However, they can provide contact information for the appropriate district office in your area.

District offices are staffed by experts in the lending, procurement and management assistance areas, who have the responsibility of considering loan applications, offering individual management assistance and coordinating other small business services.

District offices are the contact point for small businesses needing information or assistance.

You may obtain a free **Directory of Business Development Publications** by calling (800) 368-5855. The Small Business Answer Desk (800) 368-5855 helps callers with questions on how to start and manage a business, where to get financing and other information needed to operate and expand a business.

Additional help can be obtained through Service Corps of Retired Executives (SCORE). For your nearest counseling center, call 1-800-237-GROW. These are men and women volunteers who help small businesses solve their operating problems through one-on-one counseling. They also offer workshops and training sessions. SCORE counseling is available at no cost.

Does your city have a Redevelopment Agency? This organization may offer low-interest rate loans, and buildings for sale and other money-saving services.

ASK YOURSELF

- ▶ What is an SBA loan?
- ▶ List the types of SBA loans that are available.
- ▶ How does a business owner qualify for an SBA loan?

CHAPTER EIGHT

THE ROLE OF PLANNING

PLAN FOR SUCCESS

Business and investment success are usually directly related to the effort and time that go into planning. Companies such as Apple Computer and Federal Express are hugely successful not because they were the only ones with a new concept (each had competitors with similar ideas), but primarily because they worked with detailed business plans.

A key element in these plans was an allowance for flexibility. Periods of rapid growth followed by stalls followed once again by heady growth are trying circumstances for any management team. Apple's management team underwent a celebrated change at a critical time in its history and had done it again by restructuring in 1990.

We mention both of these well-known international companies because at one point in each of their lives, they turned to SBA financing to aid in their growth. A key part of their success was their ability to show lenders and investors what they wanted to do, how much money they needed to do it and how they would be able to repay the money.

Lenders want to see that there is a close correlation between your plans and reality. If your company has been growing at a 25% annual rate in accord with your business plans, you won't have a problem. If you expect 35% annual growth in the future and your plan reflects that figure, providing for the added costs and other considerations (e.g., production facilities, marketing plans, distribution concerns), then a lender will see that your plans are based on experience and practical expectation. They will be more inclined to make the loan than if there is a discrepancy between your expected growth and considerations in your business plan.

If your business plan's projections don't bear much resemblance to your actual experience, a lender will wonder just how important a role planning plays in your business.

In your personal financial life, a budget plays a similar role. Many people get into financial difficulties due to a whimsical approach to their finances.

Likewise, without a method for keeping track of your plan, your business is like a boat without a rudder. It may be going somewhere but you're not exactly sure where.

With a budget for both personal life and for business, you know where you are, what your goals are and whether you are making progress or falling further behind. It is merely a method for keeping track. Don't underrate the value of employing proper cash management techniques at home as well as in your business.

THE IMPORTANCE OF ADVANCE PLANNING

Common sense is your best guide in advance planning. Put yourself in bankers' shoes. They are concerned with the security of their loans. They want to know that there will be sufficient cash flow to cover the necessary payments.

One of the ways they determine this is to rely on your recent income history. Have you had a stable-to-rising income over the past three to five years that is adequate to cover your living expenses, make regular loan payments and leave room for error?

If you are planning to quit your job of 20 years as a sales representative for athletic supplies in order to open your own sports store, you will be forsaking a secure income. Regardless of the fact that you have experience in athletic sales, a lender will see that you do not have a stable income history in your new profession.

Lenders want peace of mind. We have emphasized throughout this book the need to anticipate lenders' concerns. They are fourfold:

1. History and security of income

2. Willingness to pay debt

3. Value and marketability of assets

4. Secondary source of repayment

If you will retire soon but expect that you will want to pursue other ventures that will require a loan, take out the loan before retirement.

Withdrawals from IRAs or other retirement plans will show up on your tax returns. This will trigger questions from a lender.

If you are withdrawing money in anticipation of retirement, it is likely that your steady income will be less than when you are working. You will then qualify for a smaller loan.

Tax Planning

Perhaps the most obvious area in which advance planning is important is in taxes. The Tax Reform Act of 1986 greatly simplified tax brackets for individuals, reducing the tax brackets to 15%, 28% or, in some cases, 33%. However, many other parts of that tax law complicated tax planning considerations.

However, since passage of the law, many clarifications, technical corrections, and outright changes have been made to the treatment of things such as mortgage and home equity interest deductibility.

It is important that you recognize that proper tax planning can make the difference between success and failure in your business. At a very early stage in your personal or business planning, consult with a qualified tax specialist. This should be a continuing relationship since tax laws change rapidly. Failure to understand the changes and their implications for your business or personal financial affairs can be very costly.

A situation that may involve expensive tax complications is timing of asset sales. For example, you may want to show a higher income in your business next year for personal reasons to qualify for a larger loan (e.g., need to finance college education for a child).

However, the tax implications may outweigh other concerns. Tax treatment of some types of asset sales can be very complex. You wouldn't want to do something that may cost you more money than necessary by looking at only one aspect of your total financial picture. Be sure to check with your tax specialist before making any such moves.

Life Cycle Objectives

Competent financial planners spend much time on helping you define your financial goals. They realize that knowing what you want plays a vital role in determining how you arrange your financial affairs.

Personal goals vary. Perhaps you want to buy a sports car, go around the world, buy a bigger house, add a room to your home, buy a vacation home in Hawaii or provide for college education for your children. Maybe you hope to expand your business into neighboring states, go international, buy new and more efficient equipment, or many other things. Too many people and businesses take a hit-or-miss approach to their financial planning. They wind up living from paycheck to paycheck or sale to sale even as their incomes increase.

Parkinson's Law, "Expenses will increase to absorb additional income", can hold true for you. Don't let this be the case. Plan ahead.

Even if you do not anticipate needing additional money to finance a leave of absence, it is always better to arrange for its availability when you are at your strongest financially.

Naturally, your first consideration when facing a lifestyle change, such as having children, is to budget your income carefully. Do a self-audit of your spending habits. The addition of a child will mean more expenses. Don't expect to maintain your same spending habits by using a loan to conceal the subsequent income gap of one less paycheck. Cutting back on variable expenses (such as recreation and entertainment) to fund necessities (such as food, shelter and medical expenses) should be planned ahead to avoid headaches and potential angry recriminations between partners.

Business Cycle Considerations

Different businesses have different financial concerns throughout the year. Will your business be affected by the seasons (summer vs. winter, supply of materials or goods to operate at a profit, seasonal labor force)?

If your business is cyclic, you will do well to follow our advice. Prepare yourself to apply for a loan on a semiannual basis, even though you may not need one. Why? This will show you how your business is doing.

In the construction business, price fluctuations can mean the difference between making a profit or suffering a loss.

You will need to be prepared to explain to your lender the advantages that a loan to buy low-priced materials will have for your business. Show them the historical price trends. Describe what your enhanced profitability means to the lender not only in terms of being paid back on time but also in further business such as deposits.

Anticipating changes that may arise as a result of political developments is simply smart business. If zoning laws will hamper your business in one area or in a particular city, making plans to move to other areas can minimize costs. Political winds change frequently. Being unaware of their implications for your business can be suicidal.

If you are going to need money to finance a move, prepare your case and get your loan before the added expense and complications make your loan application less appealing to lenders.

1. Advance planning can pay financial dividends in terms of saved expenses.
2. Tax considerations are a primary reason for careful advance planning in all your financial affairs.
3. In most cases it is advisable to retain a tax professional to assist with your tax planning needs.
4. Personal as well as professional and financial factors can affect your need for a loan. Take these into consideration as well.
5. Take advantage of business cycles. Buy additional supplies when prices are depressed. Don't get carried away with widespread euphoria or depressed with rampant pessimism in the market.

THE ROLE OF BUDGETING

Most people at some point in their lives have experienced a shortfall between what they earn and what they spend or at least want to spend. Budgeting is simply allocating your income to cover your expenses.

Those people or companies living from paycheck to paycheck or sale to sale are never able to set aside money to buy that new house or that new equipment that will make work more efficient. If you don't plan for savings, an unexpected turn of events like an accident in which you are injured or the loss of an important customer to your business can mean financial disaster. Too late, the realization strikes that your financial affairs should have been managed in a more disciplined manner.

The first check you write should be to yourself—set aside from 5% to 10% of your paycheck or sales proceeds for savings or reinvestment.

Budget As Means of Communication

Use a budget not merely as a numerical accounting or spending checklist. It is an essential tool for communication with your life partners, whether they are family or business associates. Better communication means less friction and fewer problems.

A budget plays a threefold role in your financial affairs. It can help you plan, control and record expenditures. It is your road map to financial stability.

ASK YOURSELF

- ▶ What is the role of planning?
- ▶ How does timing affect your loan request?
- ▶ Describe the role of budgeting in requesting a loan.
- ▶ List the special loan programs.

CHAPTER EIGHT

APPENDIXES

APPENDIX I

GUIDELINE REVIEW AND CHECKLISTS FOR BORROWERS

In this Appendix we provide you with a quick recap of the most important concepts presented in the previous chapters. We have arranged the summaries under 9 headings:

1. Understanding the Loan Process
2. Preparation and Organization
3. Helping Lenders Help You
4. The SBA
5. The Non-W2 Borrower
6. Business Loans
7. Personal Loans
8. Advance Planning
9. If You Are Turned Down

In addition, we have included checklists that you should use before making a loan application. The checklists are:

1. Business plan
2. Paperwork
3. How Lenders Evaluate Loan Applications
4. Oral Presentation

Following these checklists will help you better organize your loan application.

Understanding the Loan Process

☐ Lenders want to see that you have invested your own funds before they will give you a loan.

☐ Lenders charge more when they perceive greater potential risk.

☐ Lenders prefer collateral that is liquid and widely marketable to specialized or hard-to-sell items.

- ☐ Lenders have access to independent verification of much of your credit history and current debt status through credit bureau reports.
- ☐ Rapport with your lending officer is very important. If it doesn't "feel" right, it probably isn't.
- ☐ Lenders look for four main elements:
    a. Ability to repay loan (cash flow)
    b. History of timely payment of debts
    c. Quality and liquidity of assets in case the loan fails
    d. Secondary source of repayment
- ☐ Lenders use a "scoring" system drawn from their previous experiences with different types of borrowers. The scoring system is based on financial information and personal data (number of dependents, employment record, homeowner or renter, residence stability, etc.).
- ☐ A major element of the approval process is the careful comparison of all documents for consistency.
- ☐ Secured loans are generally easier to qualify for and relatively cheaper than unsecured loans.
- ☐ Most loans are now made with variable interest rate charges that are tied to some index such as the prime rate or the Treasury bill rate.

Preparation and Organization

- ☐ Know precisely how much money you need and why.
- ☐ Be prepared with two or three years tax returns, a current balance sheet and income statement, cash flow statement, a completed loan application and, for a business, a detailed business plan.
- ☐ Good organization is a critical component of professional courtesy. Know where to quickly locate any information you may not know exactly.

- ☐ A balance sheet details your assets, liabilities, and net worth.
- ☐ An income statement itemizes your income and expenses. Expenses are expenditures that do not build up equity such as the interest portion of your car or mortgage payments.
- ☐ A cash flow statement itemizes your cash inflows and outflows without regard to equity accumulation in assets.
- ☐ You should obtain a copy of your credit report before applying for a loan.
- ☐ A thorough self-audit should be completed prior to turning any paperwork over to a lender.
    a. Point out and explain problems before the lender uncovers them. However, do not dwell on problems.
    b. If there is anything unusual about your income (it fluctuates widely, jumped significantly recently, etc.) include some explanation.
- ☐ Orient your presentation to highlight your unique strengths:
    a. financial
    b. management experience
    c. product or service
    d. location
- ☐ Practice your presentation with another person.

Helping Lenders Help You

- ☐ Be sure you are dealing with the right institution for the loan you seek.
- ☐ Consider obtaining disability coverage sufficient to cover loan payments.
- ☐ Never take your lenders for granted. Keep them advised of all important developments, positive or negative.
- ☐ All your business with a lender, not just the loan in question, is important in determining a lender's willingness to grant a loan.

- ☐ Farm property, partnerships, non-income producing real estate, and stock in closely held companies are prime examples of assets that lenders may consider potential liabilities.
- ☐ Using outside financial professionals often makes a lender feel more comfortable with the information presented.
- ☐ Anticipate potential problem areas and point them out with thorough explanations and further documentation if appropriate.
- ☐ Break down personal property to show value of especially marketable items such as coin or stamp collections, jewelry, furs, and so on.
- ☐ Do not inflate the value of property. The value of items such as autos is easily checked, and listing inflated value will cause suspicion about the balance of your information.

The SBA

- ☐ To apply for an SBA loan, you must first apply for a conventional loan. If you are turned down, ask about pursuing an SBA guaranteed loan.
- ☐ Most SBA loan applicants must meet qualification standards similar to conventional loan sources.
- ☐ Going through the SBA may be the only way to get financing for start-up operations.
- ☐ Guaranteed loans are funded by a lender and guaranteed by the SBA.
- ☐ Guaranteed loans constitute the vast majority of SBA loans.
- ☐ Direct loans are funded by the SBA but are relatively limited and available primarily to special situation borrowers (e.g., handicapped, etc.). Even then they are available only after you have been turned down by other loan sources.

- [ ] "7A" SBA-loans are for most general purposes, including:
    a. Working capital
    b. Equipment
    c. Land and building
- [ ] 502 and 504 SBA loans are tied to the economic benefits they provide the community.
- [ ] Most SBA loans charge variable interest rates ranging from prime plus 1.5% to plus 3.5%.
- [ ] The SBA assesses a guarantee fee of 1% to 2% of the amount of the loan guaranteed.
- [ ] The complexities of SBA procedures make it advisable to use a loan package when pursuing an SBA loan.
- [ ] Lenders or loan packagers typically charge from $300 to $1,700 for putting together an SBA loan proposal
- [ ] The SBA requires collateral for its loans.
- [ ] A certified SBA lender should be able to get an answer from the SBA within three days of filing an application.
- [ ] A preferred SBA lender can approve and fund an SBA loan in-house.
- [ ] The SBA is not a lender-of-last-resort welfare agency for poorly run businesses.

The Non-W2 Borrower

- [ ] A reputable loan broker can save you time and aggravation by matching you with a suitable lender and helping you present your application in the form the lender requires.
- [ ] A lender figures that a sole proprietor's income is that shown on his tax return with depreciation added back.
- [ ] A non-qualifying mortgage loan (no proof of current income) may be available with a 30% down payment.

Business Loans

- [ ] Informal financing arrangements with "Angels" (family, friends, and business associates) is a major source of funding for small businesses.
- [ ] Success in securing a loan begins with a carefully thought out business plan.
- [ ] Loan terms with some lenders are limited only by your creativity. Don't be afraid to ask for terms that suit your unique cash flow circumstances.
- [ ] Have an attorney draw up buy/sell agreements with your other principals. Fund them with life insurance if necessary.
- [ ] Explain why the loan will benefit the company in financial terms.
- [ ] Common types of business loans include line of credit, factoring, and term.
- [ ] Common security for business loans include A/R, inventory, or company assets.
- [ ] Carefully prepared financial projections detailing how the loan is going to be repaid are an important element in any business plan.
- [ ] Lenders evaluate business loan requests largely by use of financial ratios to measure liquidity, profitability, and ability to service debt.

Personal Loan Review

- [ ] Mortgage lenders will typically loan up to 80% of appraised value.
- [ ] Lenders analyze financial data to determine:
    a. Your housing ratio: a measure of monthly housing expenses divided by income. Most lenders want it to be no higher than 25% to 33%.
    b. Your debt service ratio: the total of monthly debt service payments plus housing costs divided by

monthly income. Lenders require it to be 38% to 46%. The higher your income, the higher the acceptable percentage.

- [ ] Legitimate mortgage brokers will help prepare your loan application to best meet the requirements of lenders they work with.

- [ ] Work only with proven, reputable mortgage brokers recommended by trusted friends or financial professionals.

- [ ] Work with mortgage brokers who get their fees from lenders. Do not pay a fee in advance.

- [ ] Adjustable rate mortgages carry variable rate interest charges tied to a specified index. Typical terms include a maximum 2% per year adjustment and 6% maximum over the life of the mortgage.

- [ ] When comparing adjustable and fixed rate mortgages, keep in mind that the average family sells their home in 3 to 5 years.

Advance Planning Review

- [ ] A borrower's stability is a major concern for lenders. If you anticipate a significant change in your life, consider applying for any loan you may need before making the change.

- [ ] It is more important to a lender that results correspond closely to plans than that there are prospects for huge gains.

- [ ] Tax considerations are a primary reason for careful advance planning in all your financial affairs.

    ▶ In most cases it is advisable to retain a tax professional to assist with your tax planning needs.

- [ ] Take advantage of business cycles. Buy additional supplies when prices are depressed. Don't get carried away with widespread euphoria and overextend yourself. Don't become overly depressed by rampant pessimism and sell at the worst time.

- [ ] Budgets facilitate communication among concerned parties, whether they are spouses or business partners.

If You Are Turned Down

- [ ] Request a written explanation for any credit denial.
- [ ] Are you using the right institution?
- [ ] Carefully examine your business operations to see if there are ways to increase cash flow.
- [ ] Ask if a cosigner would make a difference.
  - ▶ Ask about using a letter of credit as a form of cosigner guarantee.
- [ ] Use a CPA to review business operations and make recommendations on managing cash and credit.

Checklist: Business Plan

Key Elements of a Good Business Plan include:

- [ ] Introduction for what you are requesting (i.e., $200,000 loan for new equipment)
- [ ] Good story on the economic viability of your company
  a. Who you are
  b. Company history
  c. Description of products or services offered
  d. Analysis of competition
- [ ] Where you fit in the industry
- [ ] Management team's experience & qualifications
- [ ] Compensation information
- [ ] Description of operations
- [ ] Detailed marketing plan
- [ ] Financial Statements (CPA prepared)
  a. Balance sheet
  b. Income statement

      c. Cash flow statement

      d. Two or three years' tax returns

      e. Financial projections for five years

- [ ] Exhibits

      a. Marketing materials

      b. Relevant research reports

      c. Expert opinions

      d. Charts

Checklist: Paperwork for All Loans

- [ ] Balance sheet
- [ ] Cash flow statement
- [ ] Tax returns (two or three years)
- [ ] Copy of W2 (where applicable)
- [ ] Paycheck stub (where applicable)
- [ ] Completed loan application form
- [ ] If a business loan: Business Plan

Checklist: How Lenders Evaluate Loan Applications

- [ ] Employment (or business) history
- [ ] Current financial statements
- [ ] Balance sheet
- [ ] Cash flow statement
- [ ] Credit report
- [ ] Collateral value
- [ ] Current debts
- [ ] Financial ratios
- [ ] Business Plan
- [ ] Management experience

- ☐ Cash flow projections and ability to cover loan payments
- ☐ Industry status
- ☐ Income verification
- ☐ Past business relations
- ☐ Secondary source of repayment

Compare

- ☐ Various financial documents for consistency
- ☐ Interest income
- ☐ Interest expense
- ☐ Income past and present
- ☐ Rates of growth in income, sales, costs, and profitability

Checklist: Oral Presentation

- ☐ Practice with another person prior to meeting.
- ☐ Be prompt.
- ☐ Dress appropriately.
- ☐ Be friendly and relaxed. Smile.
- ☐ Be professional. Firm handshake.
- ☐ Be aware of your body language. Don't slouch.
- ☐ Look at the loan officer. Don't look down or away.
- ☐ Be attentive. Take notes in a nondistracting manner.
- ☐ Outline your presentation and follow it.
- ☐ Be familiar with operational and financial details. Don't be put in the position of saying "I don't know, someone else prepared that."
- ☐ Begin with the most important points: what you need, why you need it, and how it will be repaid.
- ☐ Listen carefully. Learn exactly what the lender wants.
- ☐ Respond directly to enquiries. Don't be evasive.

- ☐ If you do not know an answer, write the question down. Tell the lender when you will get the answer.
- ☐ Follow up promptly.
- ☐ Show respect and trust. Create and build on rapport.
- ☐ When speaking, make sure the lender understands what you are saying. Don't get confusingly technical. Avoid specialized industry jargon.
- ☐ Ask when you can expect a response.

APPENDIX II

KEY DOCUMENTS FILE

The following details what each person or household should put together in a file with a copy stored in a safe place away from your home (i.e., with your lawyer or CPA). The executor of your estate should be aware of where the file is, in case of emergency.

- DEATH LETTER
- WILLS AND ADDRESSES OF BENEFICIARIES
- POWERS OF APPOINTMENT (WILLS)
- CONSERVATORSHIPS
- PHYSICIAN'S LETTER
- TRUSTS AND ADDRESSES OF BENEFICIARIES
- INSURANCE POLICIES (FACING PAGE ONLY)
- SUMMARY OF EMPLOYEE BENEFITS
- EMPLOYMENT CONTRACTS
- DEEDS
- PROPERTY IMPROVEMENTS
- BEARER BONDS
- STOCK CERTIFICATES
- PARTNERSHIP AGREEMENTS
- DEBT INSTRUMENTS - LOAN CONTRACTS
- BIRTH CERTIFICATES
- SOCIAL SECURITY CARD
- PASSPORT
- MARRIAGE CERTIFICATE
- ADOPTION CERTIFICATE

DIVORCE DECREES

ANNUITIES

BANK ACCOUNT LIST INCLUDING SAFE DEPOSIT BOX(ES)

LEASEHOLD OBLIGATIONS

COPYRIGHTS

PATENTS

MINERAL RIGHTS

GIFT TAX RETURNS

AGREEMENTS CONCERNING BUSINESS INTERESTS:

1. BUY-SELL
2. RIGHT OF FIRST REFUSAL

ANTENUPTIAL OR OTHER MARITAL AGREEMENTS

LIST OF ATTORNEY, ACCOUNTANT, INSURANCE AGENT, PHYSICIANS AND SECURITIES BROKER

PINK SLIPS FOR CARS, BOATS, ETC.

FEDERAL AND STATE INCOME TAX RETURNS FOR FOUR PRIOR YEARS

APPENDIX III

SET UP YOUR FINANCIAL PROFILE ON A SPREADSHEET
by John W. Price, Ph.D.

The most efficient method to organize and present your financial profile is to use a computer-ized spreadsheet. Today, while these are many excellent programs, the most widely used are Lotus 1-2-3™ for the PC and Microsoft Excel™ for the Macintosh.

Spreadsheets are not only easy to use, they are fully customizable. So if the templates presented below do not completely fit your needs, you will find it a straightforward task to embellish the basic model.

For both Lotus and Excel the format is similar. They differ only in the syntax of the formulas, and the conventions regarding the formatting of the document.

Lotus on the PC

The balance sheet appears at the top of the first page of the profile. As described in Chapter II, it lists your Assets, Liabilities, and Net Worth at a point in time. Note carefully that all values put into your balance sheet will be fair market values rather than historical cost. For example, your residence should be valued at what you could reasonably expect to sell it for, and not the cost of purchase.

Directly below the Asset column is the value of the Current Ratio. This figure should be well above 1; it calculates the ratio of your liquid assets to your short-term liquid liabilities.

The Income Statement shows sources of annual income on the left side, and expenses on the right. Your surplus or net income is an important financial signal for many reasons, one of which is that generally it is the largest source of your cash flow (along with investing and financing activities).

**YOUR NAME GOES HERE
PERSONAL FINANCIAL PROFILE
@NOW**

ASSETS		LIABILITIES & NET WORTH	
Cash - Sch. 1	+B70	Notes Payable-Current - Sch. 5	+B139
Short Term Invest.- Sch. 2	+B80	Mortgages-Current - Sch. 6	+B156
Other Current Assets	0	Credit Cards	0
		Other Current Liabilities	0
Total Current Assets	@SUM(B9..B17)	Total Current Liabilities	@SUM(E9..E17)
		Notes Payable-Long Term - Sch. 7	+B141
Real Estate - Sch. 3	+G96	Mortgages-Long Term - Sch. 8	+B158
Cash Value Life Insurance	0	Vehicle Loans	0
Stocks and Bonds - Sch. 4	+B111	Other Long-Term Liabilities	0
Retirement Assets	0		
Other Long-Term Assets		Total Liabilities	@SUM(E18..E30)
		Personal Net Worth	+B35-E31
Total Assets	@SUM(B18..B34)	Total Liabilities & Net Worth	+E31+E33
	=======		=========
Current Ratio	+B18/E18		

ANNUAL BUDGETED INCOME AND EXPENSES

INCOME		EXPENSES	
Gross Salary - Sch. 9	+B171	Annual Mortgage Payments	+G97
Rentals-Net Cash Flow	0	Taxes & Licenses - Sch. II	+B192
Dividends	0	Interest Expense	0
Interest - Sch. 10	+B180	Personal Expense - Sch. 12	+B205
Other Income	+B169	Other Expenses	0
Total Annual Income	@SUM(B46..B55)	Total Annual Expenses	@SUM(E44..E55)
Net Excess/(Shortage)	+B46-E56		
	=========		

Schedule 1 - Cash Assets

Total Cash   @SUM(B64..B69)

Schedule 2 - Short-Term Investments

Total S/T Investments   @SUM(B74..B79)

Schedule 3 - Real Estate

	Property #1	Property #2	Property #3	Totals
Type of Property	Personal Residence			
Address				
Date of Purchase				
Cost Plus Improvements				@SUM(C89..E89)
Mortgage Maturity Date				
Lender				
Loan Number				
Amount - First Mortgage				@SUM(C93..E93)
Amount - Second Mortgage				@SUM(C94..E94)
Amount - Third Mortgage				@SUM(C95..E95)
Est. Fair Market Value				@SUM(C96..E96)
Annual Mortgage Payment				@SUM(C97..E97)
Annual Rental Income				@SUM(C98..E98)

Schedule 4 - Stock & Bonds

Total Stocks & Bonds   @SUM(B102..B110)

Schedules 5 and 6 - Notes Payable

Total Notes Payable	@SUM(B123..B129)
Current Notes Payable	
Total Current Payable	@SUM(B134..B138)
Long Term Notes Payable	+B130-B139

Schedules 6 and 7 - Mortgage Debt

First Mortgates-Sch 3	+G93
Second Mortgages-Sch 3	+G94
Third Mortgages-Sch 3	+G95
Total Mortgages	@SUM(B148..B151)
Estimated Current Portion	
(12% of total)	+B152*0.12
Estimated Long Term	
(88% of total)	+B152*0.88
Total Mortgages	@SUM(B156..B159)

Schedule 9 - Gross Salary

Total Salary	@SUM(B163..B168)

Schedule 10 - Interest Income

Total Interest	@SUM(B172..B177)

Schedule 11 - Taxes & Licenses

Total Taxes &
Licenses   @SUM(B182..B188)

Schedule 12 - Personal Expenses

Food
Home Expenditures
Clothing
Entertainment
Transportation
Other
Total Personal
Expenses   @SUM(B192..B201)

Credit Cards Used in Business:

Issued by	Type	Card Number	Issue Date
_____	_____	_____	_____
_____	_____	_____	_____
_____	_____	_____	_____
_____	_____	_____	_____
_____	_____	_____	_____
_____	_____	_____	_____

Credit Cards Used in Household:

Issued by	Type	Card Number	Issue Date
_____	_____	_____	_____
_____	_____	_____	_____
_____	_____	_____	_____
_____	_____	_____	_____
_____	_____	_____	_____
_____	_____	_____	_____

Personal Information

Name _____

Home Address _____

Home Phone _____

Business Phone _____

Birth Date _____

Social Security Number _____

Occupation _____

Employer _____

Years Employed _____

Business Address _____

The categories on the lead page show only totals. The 12 most important categories are control accounts which have detail schedules that appear on the following pages. (Of course you can create a new schedule, and put the formula in the proper cell on the lead page to display the total.)

The final portion of the profile allows you to include information which, while it is of a non-financial nature, would be relevant to a lender. You should also add any other items that you feel would strengthen your borrower position.

Most households will want to spend extra time entering figures for Schedule 3, which is for your real estate. Residential and rental property is the most important investment for most people. Note also that Schedules 5 through 8 break down your debt into Current versus Long-term for your balance sheet and Current Ratio.

The present structure of the spreadsheet will allow printing on narrow (8.5 inch) paper only if condensed print is used. Using a wider typeface (10 pitch) or adding more columns would imply you would have to use wide paper for printouts.

Procedures

- ▶ Begin by creating the spreadsheet on your computer. Don't forget to increase the width of the wider columns.
- ▶ Enter line items for all Schedules. Round figures to the nearest dollar.
- ▶ Recalculate all formulas by striking the F9 key (assuming you have chosen the default as Manual Recalculation).
- ▶ Go to the first page; enter totals for non-schedule items.
- ▶ Press F9 again. Save the file as you normally would.
- ▶ Print a copy. (You may want to quickly create a print macro, as it is likely you will have to print many copies.)
- ▶ Proofread it. Analyze from a lender's viewpoint.
- ▶ Go back and edit parts that should be improved.
- ▶ If one of your paper copies will be given to a lender, make sure it looks as professional as possible, i.e., use a dark ribbon and high-quality paper.

Excel on the Macintosh

The format of the financial profile, and the user procedures are basically the same for the Macintosh. The main difference is the formulas. This is readily seen when we view the Financial Profile as set up on an Excel spreadsheet.

Other possibilities

If you are using some other spreadsheet such as Excel™ - PC, Supercalc™, Quattro Pro™, or PlanPerfect™, the procedures are similar (Indeed the formulas using Excel on a PC are virtually the same as for the Mac.)

What about graphs? One of the most powerful features of these electronic spreadsheets is the option to quickly display financial trends in chart format. For example, you could create a pie-chart for your expenditures.

For most borrowers, however, it is not worthwhile to include graphics. Lenders generally are "number-crunchers" who will look closely at figures and ratios, and would likely pass on your graphs.

YOUR NAME GOES HERE
PERSONAL FINANCIAL PROFILE
@NOW

ASSETS		LIABILITIES & NET WORTH	
Cash - Sch. 1	=B70	Notes Payable-Current - Sch. 5	=B139
Short Term Invest.- Sch. 2	=B80	Mortgages-Current - Sch. 6	=B156
Other Current Assets	0	Credit Cards	0
		Other Current Liabilities	0
	_____		_____
Total Current Assets	=SUM(B9:B17)	Total Current Liabilities	=SUM(E9:E17)
Real Estate - Sch. 3	=G96	Notes Payable-Long Term - Sch. 7	=B141
Cash Value Life Insurance	0	Mortgages-Long Term - Sch. 8	=B158
Stocks and Bonds - Sch. 4	=B111	Vehicle Loans	0
Retirement Assets	0	Other Long-Term Liabilities	0
Other Long-Term Assets			_____
		Total Liabilities	=SUM(E18:E30)
		Personal Net Worth	=B35-E31
	_____		_____
Total Assets	=SUM(B18:B34)	Total Liabilities & Net Worth	=E31+E33
	==============		=========

ANNUAL BUDGETED INCOME AND EXPENSES

INCOME		EXPENSES	
Gross Salary - Sch. 9	=B171	Annual Mortgage Payments	=G97
Rentals-Net Cash Flow	0	Taxes & Licenses — Schedule 11	=B192
Dividends	0	Interest Expense	0
Interest - Sch. 10	=B180	Personal Expense - Sch. 12	=B205
Other Income	=B169	Other Expenses	0
	_____		_____
Total Annual Income	=SUM(B46:B55)	Total Annual Expenses	=SUM(E44:E55)
Net Excess/(Shortage)	=B46-E56		
	=========		

APPENDIX THREE: SET UP YOUR FINANCIAL PROFILE ON A SPREADSHEET

Schedule 1 - Cash Assets

Total Cash =SUM(B64:B69)

Schedule 2 - Short Term Investments

Total S/T Investments =SUM(B74:B79)

Schedule 3 - Real Estate

	Property #1	Property #2	Property #3	Totals
Type of Property	Personal Residence			
Address				
Date of Purchase				
Cost Plus Improvements				=SUM(C89:E89)
Mortgage Maturity Date				
Lender				
Loan Number				
Amount - First Mortgage				=SUM(C93.:E93)
Amount - Second Mortgage				=SUM(C94:E94)
Amount - Third Mortgage				=SUM(C95:E95)
Est. Fair Market Value				=SUM(C96:E96)
Annual Mortgage Payment				=SUM(C97:E97)
Annual Rental Income				=SUM(C98:E98)

Schedule 4- Stock & Bonds

Total Stocks & Bonds =SUM(B102:B110)

Schedules 5 and 6 - Notes Payable

Total Notes Payable =SUM(B123:B129)

Current Notes Payable

Total Current Payable =SUM(B134:B138)
Long Term Notes Payable =B130-B139

Schedules 6 and 7 - Mortgage Debt

First Mortgages-Sch 3 =G93
Second Mortgages-Sch 3 =G94
Third Mortgages-Sch 3 =G95

Total Mortgages =SUM(B148:B151)

Estimated Current Portion
(12% of total) =B152*0.12
Estimated Long Term
 (88% of total) =B152*0.88

Total Mortgages =SUM(B156:B159)

Schedule 9 - Gross Salary

Total Salary =SUM(B163:B168)

Schedule 10 - Interest Income

Total Interest =SUM(B172:B177)

Schedule 11 - Taxes & Licenses

Total Taxes &
Licenses   =SUM(B182:B188)

Schedule 12 - Personal Expenses

Food
Home Expenditures
Clothing
Entertainment
Transportation
Other
Total Personal
Expenses   =SUM(B192:B201)

Credit Cards Used in Business:

Issued by	Type	Card Number	Issue Date
_____	_____	_____	_____
_____	_____	_____	_____
_____	_____	_____	_____
_____	_____	_____	_____
_____	_____	_____	_____

Credit Cards Used in Household:

Issued by	Type	Card Number	Issue Date
_____	_____	_____	_____
_____	_____	_____	_____
_____	_____	_____	_____
_____	_____	_____	_____
_____	_____	_____	_____

Personal Information

Name _____

Home Address _____

Home Phone _____

Business Phone _____

Birth Date _____

Social Security Number _____

Occupation _____

Employer _____

Years Employed _____

Business Address _____

APPENDIX IV
LIST OF BANKS IN THE SBA CLP/PLP PROGRAM

ALABAMA

Anniston	First Alabama Bank
Anniston	SouthTrust Bank of Calhoun County
Birmingham	AmSouth Bank, N.A.
Birmingham	*Central Bank of the South
Birmingham	First Alabama Bank of Birmingham
Birmingham	National Bank of Commerce of Birmingham
Birmingham	SouthTrust Bank of Alabama-Birmingham, N.A.
Decatur	SouthTrust Bank of Decatur
Florence	First National Bank of Florence
Guntersville	The Home Bank
Huntsville	South Trust Bank of Huntsville
Montgomery	The First Alabama Bank of Montgomery, N.A.
Montgomery	South Trust Bank, N.A.
Opelika	Farmers National Bank
Selma	Peoples Bank & Trust Co.
Sheffield	Bank Independent

ALASKA

Anchorage	*Key Bank of Alaska
Anchorage	First National Bank of Alaska
Fairbanks	First National Bank of Fairbanks

ARIZONA

Phoenix	*The Arizona Bank
Phoenix	Liberty Bank
Phoenix	First Interstate Bank of Arizona, N.A.

*Preferred Lender

Phoenix	*Thunderbird Bank
Phoenix	*The Valley National Bank of Arizona
Scottsdale	Ranch National Bank
Tempe	Rio Salado Bank

ARKANSAS

Batesville	First National Bank
Fayetteville	McIlroy Bank & Trust
Fort Smith	City National Bank of Fort Smith
Fort Smith	Merchants National Bank of Fort Smith
Harrison	First National Bank of Harrison
Hot Springs	*First National Bank of Hot Springs
Jonesboro	Citizens Bank of Jonesboro
Little Rock	First Commercial Bank, N.A.
Little Rock	Worthen Bank and Trust Company
North Little Rock	The Twin City Bank
Rogers	First National Bank
Texarkana	*Commercial National Bank of Texarkana

CALIFORNIA

Anaheim	Landmark Bank
Anaheim	Pacific Inland Bank
Bakersfield	*San Joaquin Bank
Buena Park	Mercury Savings and Loan Association
Carlsbad	Bank of LaCosta
Carlsbad	Capital Bank of Carlsbad
Citrus Heights	Sunrise Bank
Covina	*California State Bank
Dana Point	Dana Niguel Bank, N.A.
Encino	Bank of Industry
Eureka	Bank of Loleta

Fairfield	Suisun Valley Bank
Fresno	Bank of Fresno
Huntington Beach	*Mercury Savings & Loan
Los Angeles	First Interstate Bank of California
Los Angeles	*Government Funding CALBIDCO
Los Angeles	Liberty National Bank
Los Angeles	Mid City Bank
Los Angeles	*National Bank of California
Modesto	Modesto Banking Co.
Monterey	Monterrey Co. Bank
Paramount	*Mechanics National Bank
Redding	North Valley Bank
Redding	Tri-Counties Bank
Roseville	Sunrise Bank of California
Sacramento	*The Money Store Investment Corporation
Sacramento	*Sacramento Commercial Bank
Sacramento	Sacramento First National Bank
San Diego	*Bank of Commerce
San Diego	First National Bank
San Diego	ITT Small Business Finance Corp.
San Diego	*San Diego Trust & Savings Bank
San Francisco	Commercial Bank of San Francisco
San Francisco	*First Capital
San Jose	*Pacific Western
San Leandro	Bay Bank of Commerce
San Luis Obispo	*First Bank of San Luis Obispo
Santa Ana	Sunwest Bank
Santee	Cuyamaca Bank
Solana Beach	Torrey Pines Bank

Truckee	*Truckee River Bank
Tustin	Eldorado Bank
Whittier	*Bank of America

COLORADO

Aurora	Colorado National Bank - Aurora
Aurora	*The Money Store Investment Corp.
Denver	*Southwestern Commercial Capital
Englewood	*Republic National Bank of Englewood
Englewood	Southwestern Commercial Capital, Inc.
Glenwood Springs	Central Bank of Glenwood Springs
Grand Junction	Central Bank of Grand Junction
Grand Junction	First National Bank-North
Greeley	United Bank of Greeley
Hotchkiss	The First State Bank of Hotchkiss
Littleton	United Bank of Littleton
Montrose	IntraWest Bank of Montrose, N.A.
Pueblo	Pueblo Bank & Trust Co.

CONNECTICUT

Bridgeport	Citytrust
Hamden	*American National Bank
Hartford	The Connecticut Bank and Trust Company
Hartford	Connecticut National Bank
Hartford	United Bank and Trust Company
Waterbury	Bank of Boston, Connecticut (Colonial)

DELAWARE

Wilmington	Mellon Bank (DE) NA

DISTRICT OF COLUMBIA
(Washington, D.C. SMSA)

Alexandria, VA	*Crestar Bank
Falls Church, VA	The Washington Bank
Silver Spring	Signet Bank
Washington, D.C.	Allied Lending Corporation
Washington, D.C.	The National Bank of Washington

FLORIDA

Bradenton	First National Bank of Florida
Coral Gables	*Professional Savings Bank
Ft. Walton Bch	First National Bank and Trust
Jacksonville	Barnett Bank of Jacksonville, N.A.
Jacksonville	First Guaranty Bank & Trust Company
Jacksonville	Five Points Guaranty Bank
Marianna	Citizens State Bank
North Miami Beach	First Western SBLC, Inc.
Orlando	Sun Bank, N.A.
Panama City	*Bay Bank & Trust Company
Panama City	*Amsouth Bank of Florida
Panama City	*Gulf American SBL, Inc.
Panama City	Security Federal Savings Bank of Florida
West Palm Beach	Bay Savings Bank

GEORGIA

Atlanta	Buckhead Bank
Atlanta	*The Business Development Corporation of Georgia
Atlanta	The Citizens & Southern National Bank
Atlanta	Commercial Bank of Georgia
Atlanta	Decatur Federal Savings & Loan

Atlanta	Fidelity National Bank
Atlanta	First Atlanta Bank
Atlanta	*Fulton Federal Savings & Loan Association
Atlanta	Bank South, N.A.
Atlanta	ITT Small Business Financial Corp.
Atlanta	The Merchants Bank
Atlanta	*Southern Federal Savings & Loan Association of GA
Atlanta	Standard Chartered Bank
Atlanta	The Summit National Bank
Atlanta	Trust Company Bank
Atlanta	*North Carolina National Bank
Augusta	*Bankers First
Byron	Middle Georgia Bank
Chatsworth	Cohutta Banking company
Fort Valley	First South Bank
Gainesville	First National Bank of Gainesville
Mableton	Community Bank & Trust
Marietta	*The Chattahoochee Bank
Riverdale	Tara Bank
Savannah	*AmeriBank

HAWAII

Honolulu	*Bank of Hawaii
Honolulu	Central Pacific Bank
Honolulu	City Bank
Honolulu	First Hawaiian Bank

IDAHO

Boise	*First Security Bank of Idaho
Boise	*Idaho First National Bank
Boise	American Bank of Commerce

ILLINOIS

Bellwood	Bank of Bellwood
Benton	*United Illinois Bank of Benton
Champaign	Marine Bank of Champaign
Chicago	*Albany Bank and Trust Company, N.A.
Chicago	Colonial Bank and Trust Company
Chicago	Columbia National Bank of Chicago
Chicago	Hyde Park Bank & Trust Company
Chicago	ITT Small Business Finance Corporation
Chicago	Metropolitan Bank and Trust Company
Chicago	Midtown Bank and Trust Company
Chicago	Seaway National Bank of Chicago
Chicago	*The South Shore Bank of Chicago
Chicago	South Central Bank & Trust
Danville	Palmer American National Bank
East Peoria	*Community Bank of Greater Peoria
Elgin	Union National Bank & Trust of Elgin
Freeport	State Bank of Freeport
Harwood Heights	Parkway Bank & Trust Company
Joliet	*First Midwest Bank/Joliet
Melrose	Melrose Park National Bank
Mt. Zion	Mt. Zion State Bank
Monmouth	Security Savings & Loan Association
Peoria	Commercial National Bank of Peoria
Peoria	Jefferson Trust and Savings Bank of Peoria
Pekin	First State Bank of Pekin
Rockford	First National Bank and Trust Company of Rockford
Rockford	Northwest Bank of Rockford
Rockford	United Bank of Illinois, N.A.
Springfield	Marine Bank of Springfield

Urbana	*Busey First National Bank
Wilmette	Edens Plaza State Bank

INDIANA

Covington	Bank of Western Indiana
Fort Wayne	Lincoln National Bank & Trust Company of Fort Wayne
Fort Wayne	Summit Bank
Indianapolis	Bank One Indianapolis
Indianapolis	The Indiana National Bank
Merrillville	Bank One, Merrillville
Muncie	American National Bank & Trust Co. of Muncie
South Bend	First Source Bank of South Bend
South Bend	Trustcorp Bank
South Bend	Valley American Bank & Trust Co.

IOWA

Cedar Rapids	Brenton Bank and Trust Company of Cedar Rapids
Cedar Rapids	*The Merchants National Bank of Cedar Rapids
Cedar Rapids	United State Bank
Charles City	Citizens National Bank
Davenport	*Davenport Bank and Trust Company
Davenport	First Trust & Savings Bank
Davenport	Northwest Bank and Trust Company
Denison	Crawford County Trust & Savings Bank
Des Moines	Bankers Trust Company
Des Moines	Brenton National Bank of Des Moines
Des Moines	Hawkeye Bank & Trust of Des Moines
Des Moines	*Norwest Bank Des Moines, N.A.
Des Moines	*Valley National Bank
Dubuque	Dubuque Bank and Trust Company
Fort Dodge	First American State Bank

Fort Dodge	Norwest Bank Fort Dodge, N.A.
Iowa City	Iowa State Bank and Trust Company
Maquoketa	Maquoketa State Bank
Marion	Farmers State Bank
Newton	Jasper County Savings Bank
Sergeant Bluff	Pioneer Bank
Sioux Center	American State Bank
Sioux City	Norwest Bank Sioux City N.A.
Sioux City	*Security National Bank
Spencer	First Interstate Bank of Spencer, N.A.
Urbandale	First Interstate Bank of Urbandale
West Des Moines	First National Bank of West Des Moines
West Des Moines	*West Des Moines State Bank
West Union	The First National Bank of West Union

KANSAS

Dodge City	Fidelity State Bank & Trust Company
Dodge City	First National Bank and Trust Company in Dodge City
Hutchinson	Hutchinson National Bank & Trust Company
Kansas City	Guaranty State Bank & Trust
Liberal	*First National Bank
Newton	Midland National Bank
Neodesha	First National Bank of Neodesha
Olathe	First National Bank
Olathe	Bank IV Olathe
Overland Park	Metcalf State Bank
Overland Park	Overland Park State Bank & Trust Co.
Shawnee	*United Kansas Bank & Trust
Topeka	Commerce Bank and Trust
Topeka	The Merchants National Bank of Topeka
Ulysses	Grant County State Bank

Wichita	American National Bank
Wichita	*Central Bank & Trust
Wichita	*First National Bank in Wichita
Wichita	*Bank IV Wichita

KENTUCKY

Ashland	First American Bank
Bowling Green	American National Bank & Trust
Bowling Green	Bowling Green Bank & Trust
Bowling Green	Citizens National Bank of Bowling Green
Covington	Kentucky National Bank of Kenton County
Danville	Bank of Danville
Florence	The Fifth Third Bank
Lexington	Central Bank
Lexington	First Security National Bank & Trust Co.
Louisville	Citizens Fidelity Bank & Trust Co.
Louisville	First National Bank of Louisville
Monticello	First State Bank
Mount Sterling	Exchange Bank of Kentucky
Murray	Peoples Bank of Murray
Paducah	Peoples First National Bank of Paducah
Pikeville	Pikeville National Bank & Trust Company

LOUISIANA

Abbeville	Gulf Coast Bank
Baton Rouge	*Capital Bank & Trust Company
Baton Rouge	City National Bank
Baton Rouge	Premier Bank
Lafayette	Acadiana National Bank
Lafayette	Guaranty Bank & Trust Co.
Lafayette	First National Bank

Lafayette	MidSouth National Bank
Metairie	Hibernia National Bank in Jefferson Parish
Metairie	Jefferson Guaranty Bank
Monroe	American Bank
Monroe	The Ouachita National Bank in Monroe
New Orleans	First National Bank of Commerce
Plattonville	Bayoulands Bank
Shreveport	First National Bank of Shreveport

MAINE

August	*Key Bank of Central Maine
Bar Harbor	The First National Bank of Bar Harbor
Portland	Casco Northern Bank, N.A. (Southern Division)
Portland	Key Bank of Southern Maine
Portland	Maine National Bank
Portland	Fleet Bank of Maine

MARYLAND

Baltimore	First National Bank of Maryland
Baltimore	*Maryland National Bank
Baltimore	*Signet Bank

MASSACHUSETTS

Boston	*Bank of Boston
Boston	Bank of New England-NA
Boston	Boston-Massachusetts Business Development Corp.
Boston	*Shawmut Bank of Boston
Fitchburg	First Safety Fund National Bank
Hyannis	*Cape Cod Bank and Trust Company
Lawrence	Arlington Trust Company
Peabody	*Bank of New England-Essex

Pittsfield	Berkshire Bank and Trust Company
Pittsfield	First Agricultural Bank
Quincy	Bank of New England-Hancock
Rockland	Rockland Trust Company
Springfield	*Bank of New England-West
Worcester	Commerce Bank and Trust Company
Worcester	*Bank of New England-Worcester
Worcester	Shawmut Worcester County Bank, N.A.

MICHIGAN

Detroit	National Bank of Detroit
Kalamazoo	First of America Bank-Michigan, N.A.
Kalamazoo	Old Kent Bank of Kalamazoo
Kentwood	*United Bank of Michigan
Midland	*Chemical Bank & Trust Company
Traverse City	The Empire National Bank of Traverse City

MINNESOTA

Hibbing	Merchants & Miners State Bank
Minneapolis	*First Bank National Association
Minneapolis	ITT Small Business Finance Corp.
Rochester	Norwest Bank Rochester
St. Cloud	*First American National Bank of St. Cloud
St. Cloud	Zapp National Bank
Young America	State Bank of Young America

MISSISSIPPI

Batesville	Batesville Security Bank
Biloxi	The Jefferson Bank
Biloxi	Metropolitan National Bank
Jackson	*Deposit Guaranty National Bank

Jackson	Trustmark National Bank
Picayune	First National Bank of Picayune
Starkville	National Bank of Commerce of Mississippi
Tupelo	Bank of Mississippi

MISSOURI

Bonne Terre	Commerce Bank of Bonne Terre
Clinton	First National Bank of Clinton
Columbia	Boone County National Bank of Columbia
Columbia	*First National Bank & Trust Company
Cuba	Peoples Bank of Cuba
Festus	Commerce Bank of Jefferson City
Jefferson City	*The Central Trust Bank
Joplin	First National Mercantile Bank and Trust Co.
Kahoka	Commerce Bank of Kahoka
Kansas City	Boatmen's First National Bank of Kansas City
Kansas City	United Missouri Bank of Kansas City, N.A.
Malden	First Community Bank
Moberly	City Bank and Trust Company of Moberly
O'Fallon	Mark Twain St. Charles County Bank, N.A.
Poplar Bluff	Mercantile Bank of Poplar Bluff
Poplar Bluff	First National Bank of Poplar Bluff
Sikeston	First National Bank of Sikeston
Springfield	*The Boatmen's National Bank of Springfield
Springfield	Commerce Bank of Springfield
Springfield	*First City National Bank
Springfield	Mercantile Bank of Springfield
Springfield	United Bank of Missouri
St. Louis	American Bank of St. Louis
St. Louis	Boatmen's National Bank of St. Louis

St. Louis	Centerre Bank
St. Louis	Commerce Bank of St. Louis
St. Louis	*Mercantile Trust Company, N.A.
St. Louis	Missouri State Bank and Trust Company
St. Louis	United Missouri Bank of St. Louis, N.A.
St. Peters	Commerce Bank of St. Charles County

MONTANA

Billings	First Bank-Billings
Billings	*First Interstate Bank
Billings	Norwest Bank Billings
Bozeman	First Bank-Bozeman
Bozeman	First Security Bank of Bozeman
Bozeman	Montana Bank of Bozeman
Great Falls	Norwest Bank Great Falls
Helena	First Bank Helena
Helena	Valley Bank of Helena
Kalispell	*Norwest Bank Kalispell, NA
Kalispell	Valley Bank of Kalispell
Missoula	First Bank-Southside Missoula, N.A.
Missoula	*First Security Bank of Missoula
Missoula	Montana Bank of South Missoula
Whitefish	The First National Bank of Whitefish
Whitefish	*Mountain Bank

NEBRASKA

Bellevue	First National Bank of Bellevue
Lincoln	*FirsTier Bank,Lincoln
Lincoln	National Bank of Commerce
Lincoln	*Union Bank & Trust Company

Omaha	FirsTier Bank, Omaha
Omaha	Northern Bank

NEVADA

Las Vegas	Continental National Bank
Las Vegas	*Valley Bank of Nevada
Las Vegas	*First Interstate Bank of Nevada, N.A.
Reno	Nevada National Bank

NEW HAMPSHIRE

Manchester	BankEast
Manchester	Bank of New Hampshire, N.A.
Manchester	Merchants National Bank of Manchester

NEW JERSEY

Bloomfield	Midlantic National Bank
Burlington	*First Fidelity Bank, N.A. South Jersey
Flemington	The Town and Country Bank
Jackson	*Garden State Bank
Lodi	*National Community Bank of New Jersey
Newark	*First Fidelity Bank, NA
North Plainfield	*North Plainfield State Bank
Sommerville	ITT Small Business Finance Corporation
Union	*The Money Store of New York

NEW MEXICO

Albuquerque	The Bank of Albuquerque
Albuquerque	Banquest National Bank
Albuquerque	First Interstate of Albuquerque
Albuquerque	*The First National Bank of Albuquerque
Albuquerque	Sunwest Bank of Albuquerque

Albuquerque	United New Mexico Bank at Albuquerque
Albuquerque	Western Bank
Carlsbad	Western Commerce Bank
Clovis	Western Bank of Clovis
Farmington	Western Bank
Las Cruces	Bank of the Rio Grande, N.A.
Las Cruces	*United New Mexico Bank at Las Cruces
Rio Rancho	United New Mexico at Rio Rancho
Ruidoso	Ruidoso State Bank

NEW YORK

Albany	*New York Business Development Corporation
Albany	Norstar Bank of Upstate, N.Y.
Bath	The Bath National Bank
Buffalo	Key Bank of Western New York, NA
Buffalo	*Norstar Bank
Buffalo	*Manufacturers and Traders Trust Company
Buffalo	*Marine Midland Bank, N.A.
Glens Falls	Glens Falls National Bank and Trust Company
Glens Falls	The First National Bank of Glens Falls
Huntington	*Chemical Bank
Ithaca	Thompkins County Trust Company
New York City	*Chase Manhattan Bank, N.A.
New York City	*Citibank, N.A.
New York City	Manufacturers Hanover Trust Company
New York City	*National Westminster Bank
Rochester	Chase Lincoln First Bank, N.A.
Rosslyn Heights	*The Money Store Investment Corporation
Schenectady	The Schenectady Trust Company
Syracuse	Key Bank of Central New York

THE LOAN BOOK

Syracuse	*Marine Midland Bank
Syracuse	Merchants National Bank & Trust Company
Watertown	Jefferson National Bank
Watertown	Key Bank of Northern New York, N.A.

NORTH CAROLINA

Charlotte	First Union National Bank of North Carolina
Charlotte	NCBN National Bank of North Carolina
Charlotte	Southeastern Savings & Loan Company
Lumberton	Southern National Bank of North Carolina
Rocky Mount	Peoples Bank & Trust Company
Rocky Mount	The Planters National Bank & Trust Company
Whiteville	United Carolina Bank
Wilson	Branch Banking & Trust Company
Winston-Salem	*Wachovia Bank & Trust Company, N.A.

NORTH DAKOTA

Grand Forks	First National Bank in Grand Forks
Minot	First Western Bank of Minot
West Fargo	West Fargo State Bank
Williston	American State Bank and Trust Company of Williston

OHIO

Akron	Bank One, Akron, NA
Akron	First National Bank of Ohio
Akron	National City Bank, Akron
Athens	Bank One, Athens, N.A.
Beachwood	Commerce Exchange Bank
Cincinnati	*The First National Bank of Cincinnati
Cleveland	AmeriTrust Company, N.A.
Cleveland	Bank One, Cleveland, N.A.

Cleveland	Society Bank
Columbus	BancOhio National Bank
Columbus	*Bank One, Columbus, N.A.
Columbus	*The Huntington National Bank
Columbus	Society Bank
Dayton	Bank One, Dayton, N.A.
Dayton	*The First National Bank
Delaware	The Delaware County Bank
Eaton	The Preble County National Bank
Lorain	Lorain National Bank
Piqua	*Citizens Heritage Bank, NA
Piqua	The Fifth Third Bank of Miami Valley
Toledo	*Mid-American National Bank & Trust Company
Toledo	Ohio Citizens Bank

OKLAHOMA

Oklahoma City	Brookwood National Bank
Oklahoma City	First Interstate Bank of Oklahoma
Oklahoma City	Rockwell Bank, N.A.
Oklahoma City	*Southwestern Commercial Capital, Inc.
Shawnee	Federal National Bank & Trust
Stillwater	*Stillwater National Bank and Trust Company
Tonkawa	*First National Bank of Tonkawa
Tulsa	Security Bank

OREGON

Portland	*First Interstate Bank of Oregon, N.A.
Portland	Key Bank of Oregon

PENNSYLVANIA

Altoona	Mid-State Bank & Trust Company
Erie	*Marine Bank

Ft. Washington	*The Money Store Investment
Hermitage	*First National Bank of Mercer County
Johnstown	United States National Bank in Johnstown
Laceyville	Grange National Bank of Wyoming County
Morrisville	*Bucks County Bank & Trust Company
Pittsburgh	Equibank, N.A.
Pittsburgh	Mellon Bank, N.A.
Pittsburgh	*Pittsburgh National Bank
Philadelphia	Mellon Bank (East), National Association
Philadelphia	Philadelphia National Bank
Reading	*Meridian Bank
Scranton	Northeastern Bank of Pennsylvania
Sharon	McDowell National Bank of Sharon
Souderton	Union National Bank & Trust Co.
Titusville	Penn Bank

RHODE ISLAND

Providence	The Citizens Trust Company
Providence	*Fleet National Bank
Providence	Old Stone Bank, a Federal Savings Bank
Providence	Peoples Bank, NA
Providence	Rhode Island Hospital Trust National Bank
Providence	Bank of New England/Old Colony

SOUTH CAROLINA

Columbia	*NCNB South Carolina
Columbia	*Business Development Corporation of South Carolina
Columbia	First Citizens Bank
Greenville	First Union National Bank
Greenville	Branch Bank & Trust
Lexington	The Lexington State Bank

Mullins	Anderson Brothers Bank
Rock Hill	Rock Hill National Bank
Sumter	The National Bank of South Carolina

SOUTH DAKOTA

Aberdeen	Norwest Bank Aberdeen, N.A.
Belle Fourche	Pioneer Bank and Trust
Brookings	First National Bank
Burke	First Fidelity Bank
Custer	First Western Bank
Huron	Farmers & Merchants Bank
Huron	Community First State Bank of Huron
Milbank	Dakota State Bank
Mitchell	Commercial Trust & Savings Bank
Philip	First National Bank
Pierre	BankWest, N.A.
Pierre	First National Bank
Rapid City	Norwest Bank South Dakota, N.A.
Rapid City	Rushmore State Bank
Sioux Falls	First Bank of South Dakota, N.A.
Sioux Falls	First National Bank in Sioux Falls
Sioux Falls	Norwest Bank Sioux Falls, N.A.
Sioux Falls	*Western Bank
Wagner	Commercial State Bank
Watertown	Norwest Bank South Dakota, National Association
Winner	Farmers State Bank
Yankton	American State Bank
Yankton	First Dakota National Bank

TENNESSEE

Chattanooga	American National Bank & Trust Company
Columbia	First Farmers & Merchants National Bank
Elizabethton	*Citizens Bank
Memphis	*Union Planters National Bank
Nashville	*First American National Bank, N.A.
Nashville	Dominion Bank of Middle Tennessee
Nashville	*Sovran Bank/Central South
Nashville	*Third National Bank

TEXAS

Amarillo	The First National Bank of Amarillo
Amarillo	Texas American Bank
Austin	The Heritage National Bank
Austin	InterFirst Bank of Austin, N.A.
Austin	The Money Store Investment Corporation
Beaumont	Parkdale Bank
Brownsville	International Bank of Commerce, N.A.
Brownsville	*Texas Commerce Bank-Brownsville
Brownwood	RepublicBank Brownwood, N.A.
Bryan	First Bank & Trust
Bryan	First City National Bank of Bryan
Buda	First Consolidated Bank - Buda, N.A.
Carrollton	City National Bank of Carrollton
Cleburne	First National Bank of Cleburne
Cleburne	First State Bank of Cleburne
College Station	United Bank of College Station, N.A.
Corpus Christi	First Commerce Bank

Corpus Christi	*First National Bank of Corpus Christi
Corpus Christi	Southwestern Commercial Capital
Dallas	The Forestwood National Bank of Dallas
Dallas	Independence Mortgage, Inc.
Dallas	Interfirst Bank-Oak Cliff
Dallas	ITT Small Business Finance Corporation
Dallas	MBank Preston
Dallas	MBank Dallas
Dallas	MBank Market Center
Dallas	Southwestern Commercial Capital, Inc.
Dallas	Stephenville Bank & Trust Co.
El Paso	Cielo Vista Bank
El Paso	InterFirst Bank, El Paso, N.A.
El Paso	*MBank El Paso, N.A.
Fort Worth	Fort Worth State Bank
Fort Worth	Texas American Bank
Granbury	Community Bank
Harlingen	Harlingen National Bank
Harlingen	The Harlingen State Bank
Harlingen	First Republic Bank
Henderson	RepublicBank Henderson, N.A.
Houston	Allied Addicks Bank
Houston	Charter National Bank-Colonial
Houston	Charter National Bank-Houston
Houston	City National Bank
Houston	Independence Mortgage, Inc.
Houston	Lockwood National Bank
Houston	Merchant Park Bank
Lancaster	First Consolidated Bank-Pleasant Run, N.A.
Longview	*Longview Bank and Trust Company

Lubbock	American State Bank
Lubbock	Bank of West
Lubbock	First National Bank at Lubbock
Lubbock	NCNB Lubbock
Lubbock	Plans National Bank
McAllen	McAllen State Bank
McAllen	Texas Commerce Bank-McAllen, N.A.
Midland	United Bank
Missouri City	*First National Bank of Missouri City
New Braunfels	Texas Commerce Bank-New Braunfels
Odessa	Texas Bank
San Antonio	Frost Bank
San Antonio	Texas Bank
Sequin	*Southwestern Commercial Capital
Stephenville	Stephenville Bank & Trust
Temple	First National Bank of Temple
Waco	American Bank, N.A.
Waco	United Bank of Waco

UTAH

Cedar City	State Bank of Southern Utah
Logan	Cache Valley Bank
Moab	First Western National Bank
Ogden	Valley Bank & Trust
Provo	Bonneville Bank
Provo	FarWest Bank
Salt Lake City	Brighton Bank
Salt Lake City	Commercial Security Bank
Salt Lake City	The Continental Bank and Trust Company
Salt Lake City	First Interstate Bank of Utah

Salt Lake City	*First Security Bank
Salt Lake City	Guardian State Bank
Salt Lake City	*Tracy-Collins Bank and Trust Company
Salt Lake City	*Valley Bank and Trust Company
Salt Lake City	Zions First National Bank, N.A.

VERMONT

Barre	Granite Savings Bank & Trust
Brattleboro	*Vermont National Bank
Burlington	*Chittenden Trust Company
Burlington	The Howard Bank
Burlington	*The Merchant's Bank
Morrisville	*Union Bank
Randolph	*The Randolph National Bank
Rutland	Proctor Bank
St. Albans	*Franklin Lamoille Bank

VIRGINIA

Harrisonburg	Dominion Bank
Richmond	Dominion National Bank of Richmond
Richmond	*Sovran Bank, N.A.
Richmond	*Crestar

WASHINGTON

Auburn	Auburn Valley Bank
Lacey	*First Community Bank of Washington
Lynden	Peoples State Bank
Lynnwood	*City Bank
Mount Vernon	Valley Bank
Seattle	First Interstate Bank of Washington, N.A.
Seattle	Key Bank of Puget Sound
Seattle	*Security Pacific Bank

	Seattle	*Seattle-First National Bank
	Seattle	US Bank of Washington
	Snohomish	First Heritage Bank
	Spokane	Washington Trust Bank
	Wenatchee	Central Washington Bank
	Yakima	Pioneer National Bank

WEST VIRGINIA

    Huntington   *The First Huntington National Bank

WISCONSIN

	Appleton	Bank of Wisconsin
	Appleton	Valley Bank
	Brookfield	*M&I Northern Bank
	Brookfield	Bank One, Waukesha
	Brookfield	M&I Bank of Hilldale
	Brown Deer	First Bank, Brown Deer
	Eau Claire	First Interstate Bank of Wisconsin, N.A.
	Eau Claire	First Wisconsin National Bank
	Fond du Lac	*First Wisconsin National Bank of Fond du Lac
	Green Bay	Associated Kellogg
	Greenbay	First Wisconsin Bank of Greenbay
	Green Bay	University Bank
	Madison	*First Wisconsin National Bank of Madison
	Madison	Bank One, Madison
	Madison	Valley Bank Madison
	Manitowoc	Associated Manitowoc Bank
	Milwaukee	*Associated Commerce Bank
	Milwaukee	*First Wisconsin National Bank of Milwaukee
	Milwaukee	*Bank One, Milwaukee
	Sheboygan	*First Interstate Bank of Wisconsin

Sheboygan	*First Wisconsin National Bank of Sheboygan
Wausau	*First American National Bank of Wausau
Wausau	M&I First American National Bank

WYOMING

Casper	First Interstate Bank of Casper, N.A.
Casper	First Wyoming Bank-Casper
Casper	Norwest Casper Bank
Cheyenne	American National Bank
Cheyenne	*First Wyoming Bank, N.A.-Cheyenne
Laramie	First Wyoming Bank-Laramie
Rawlins	First Wyoming Bank, N.A.-Rawlins
Sheridan	Bank of Commerce

PUERTO RICO

San Juan	Banco Central Corporation
San Juan	*Banco Popular de Puerto Rico
San Juan	Government Development Bank of Puerto Rico
San Juan	Universal Trust Company

GLOSSARY

GLOSSARY

Add-on interest
The amount of interest that is added to the principal of a note. The borrower will sign a note inclusive of principal and interest and have an obligation for both.

Amortization
The systematic payment of a loan plus interest paid in the same amount for a set number of payments.

Balloon
The payment of a loan in total at some future date.

Bookkeeper
An individual without a license who claims to have certain skills in being able to summarize business transactions.

CPA
A Certified Public Accountant, licensed in the state in which the CPA resides by the Board of Accountancy, an agency of the state government who issues a test requiring a proficiency of a minimum of 75%, experience of 1-3 years in public accounting, with the completion of a college education plus higher level business curriculum courses.

Carrying costs
The costs associated with a loan, which may include interest, points, processing fee, title insurance, appraisals, etc.

Cash flow
Most closely resembling a checkbook. It records actual cash received and actual cash paid.

Commercial bank
A bank that specializes in doing business with businesses.

Commitment fee
A dollar amount charged by a lender to guarantee a borrower a loan with set terms regardless of whether the borrower takes the loan or not.

Compensating
Other business the borrower does with the balance such as checking accounts, CD's or other loans.

Cost of funds
A term used by lender to identify what it costs them for the money they lend to borrowers.

Current
A term that means some item that will be used or committed within a 12 month period from the date on which you are speaking (less than a year).

Deed of trust
A legal instrument recorded with the assessor's office that shows a lien on real property in favor of a lender.

Discounted
A charge of the full amount of interest deducted from the interest loan amount before it is advanced to the borrower.

Enrolled Agent
(EA)An individual who passes an exam that allows that individual to practice before the IRS.

Escrow
A special account set up by a third part so that a buyer and a seller can put cash and property into a transaction without fear of the other party reneging.

FDIC
A government insurance company that banks belong which protects depositors' funds up to $100,000.

FSLIC
A government insurance company that Savings & Loans belong to which protects depositors' funds up to $100,000.

Factoring
The selling of a company's account receivables to a third party for their collection, usually at a discount.

Finance company
A corporation whose stockholders lend money.

GAAP
Generally Accepted Accounting Principles. These are the guidelines set up by CPA's that all financial statements must adhere to.

Guarantee fee
See commitment fee.

Guaranty
When a second party "co-signs" on a loan for a borrower and thus takes on the responsibility for repayment of the loan.

LTV
Loan to value. It is a percentage of the loan amount to actual value of the property.

Liabilities
Those items that an entity owes someone or potentially owes someone.

Revolving line of credit
A commitment by a lender to loan up to a set amount. The loan may be taken or repaid in any amount at any time.

Long term
Reference to an item that takes over one year to become liquid.

Market value
The value that a willing buyer without influence would pay to a willing seller for an item.

Net worth
The difference between what you own and what you owe.

Points
A percentage of a loan amount that is paid up front, 1 point = 1%.

Pro forma
Projected financial statements based on the most accurate projection of the future.

Prime rate
The rate lenders charge their best borrowers.

Retail bank
Banks that specialize in individual banking.

Revolving credit
Similar to credit lines. An ability to pay a loan down or to draw the balance up (credit cards).

SBA
Small Business Administration.

Service charge
A fee charged for a service.

Short term
Reference to an item that takes less than one year to become liquid.

Signature loan
A loan that only requires a borrower's signature; no collateral is needed.

Thrift
An institution of the state or federal government that is allowed to do certain transactions. It is an institution that has a need for less capital. (That has changed as of 1989 or is going to be brought up to a par with banks). It is an institution that has less flexibility in what it can do. It can lend but does not do business transactions, i.e., checking accounts, etc., with the same freedom as a bank.

UCC filing Uniform Commercial Code
Each state has a different Uniform Commercial Code that allows individuals who wish to grant someone a loan to be secured by personal property (not real property); there is a way to verify if the personal property has been used for collateral for any other purposes. Under the UCC filing the Secretary of State has a record of the collateral issued against any loan that has already been filed with the Secretary of State and allows a total transition in allowing you to have security in a non-real estate transaction.

Vested portion of your retirement plan
The amount of money you get from your plan if you were to cash it in.